SALVATION SECURITY,
ELECTION,
and
FREE WILL

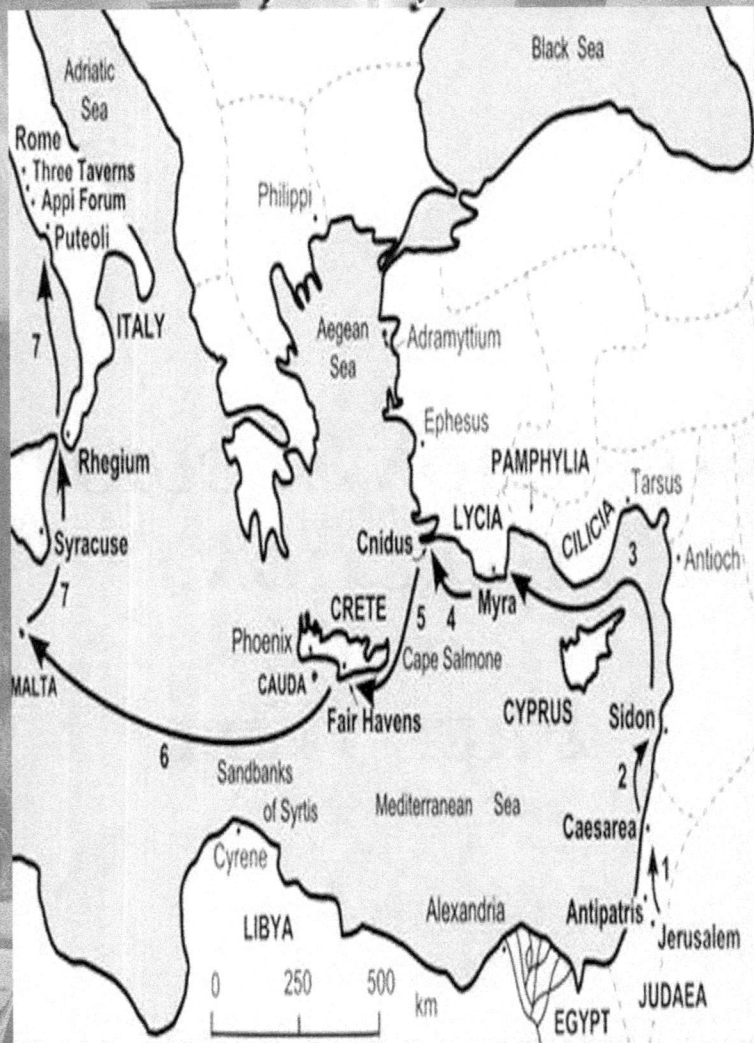

Paul's Journey to Rome

SALVATION SECURITY, ELECTION, and FREE WILL

Exploring Doctrinal Truths *via* the Book of Romans

Dr. Melonie Mayes-Tyler

NATIVE BONE Publishing

Scripture quotations are taken from the New King James Version® (NKJV) unless otherwise noted. Copyright © 1982 by Thomas Nelson. Used by permission. All rights reserved.

Published in the United States by Native Ebone' Publishing, LLC.

ISBN: 978-1-968305-01-7

Printed in the United State of America

Dedication

*To my Nana, Ocia Johnson and to my parents,
Blanchie Gray-Mayes and Robert I Mayes, Sr.
(who are all with Jesus now);
Thank you so much for training me up in the way
that I should go in the LORD.
Nana, you gave me my first Little Red verse book
which prepared me to learn and love the Psalms.
Momma, thank you for training me during BTU
and youth meetings. Because Mommy and
Daddy were educators, they instilled in me the
passion to become a life-long learner.*

*To my husband, Jermel Tyler, my siblings:
Dr. Barbara E. Mayes-Jefferson-deceased,
Dr. Jaqueline Banks
Barbara A. Mayes (Robby-deceased),
Dawn L. Mayes (Rod-deceased),
and Reginald Mayes, Sr.,
thank you all for encouraging me—pushing me
forward when I felt weary.*

*To my Pastor, Sam Holmes, Jr., thank you so
much for heeding the call of the LORD. I asked
God for a teaching Pastor and He sent you. Over
twenty-six years of amazingly, outstanding
teaching!!! I praise God for you.*

*My steps were ordered, and this was all in His
plan. Thank you for hearing my voice from Your
temple; and letting my cry reach Your ears! ALL
Praises to My ROCK!*

Testimonials

This book offers a clear and balanced look at three major doctrines: eternal security, divine election, and human free will. Dr. Mayes-Tyler breaks down complex theological ideas using Scripture, Greek word studies, and historical context. She explains how God's sovereignty works alongside human responsibility, helping readers understand terms like predestination, foreknowledge, and grace without confusion...

Whether you're new to theology or looking to deepen your understanding, this book is a valuable resource for navigating some of Christianity's most debated topics.
Katrina Ali

After reading this book and reflecting on the world which is seemingly spiraling down in spiritual darkness, I can't help but feel divine relief in knowing regardless of what is occurring around me, God is ALL I NEED!...

Salvation Security, Election, and Free Will by Dr. Melonie Mayes-Tyler is the perfect read for anyone seeking answers on how to grow in the grace and knowledge of God especially during these concerning times of uncertainty. It is clear the world is withering solely by the reckless and sinful nature of mankind but there is hope for those who believe in the promises of God...
Tracie Atkins

To God be the Glory. I am honored to have been given the opportunity to read about the topic of Salvation Security, Election and Free Will. I can truly say from a personal viewpoint that Dr. Melonie Mayes-Tyler has clearly put in much time and effort, backed by scripture, to support the overarching theme within the context of this book: God' righteousness and man's unworthiness...

As a result of reading this book, I am reassured that through Christ, my salvation is secured and my duty through free will, is now, to obey God's written word and to keep His commandments...
Dowanna Wright

TABLE OF CONTENTS

2 Tim 2:15

Be diligent to present yourself approved to God, a worker who does not need to be ashamed, rightly dividing the word of truth. NKJV

Foreword

Dr. Melonie Tyler has such a fervor for the Lord that a superficial nearness simply isn't sufficient for her. Her desire to know Him has been a lifelong pursuit. I've been blessed by her insight and her dedication to the study and her unique ability to exegete the scriptures cutting through the many shades of error going straight to a practical wisdom that is both easy to understand and doctrinally in line with some of the brightest minds who have written on the book. Romans is believed to be the greatest of Paul's writings. Martin Luther says, "It is the true masterpiece of the New Testament and the very purest gospel, which is well worth and deserving that a Christian man should not only learn it by heart word for word, but that he should daily deal with it as the daily bread of a man's soul." Dr. Tyler addresses questions that many Christians have pondered and never get a pliable answer to.

Pastor Sam Holmes, Jr.
Paradise Baptist Church

Ep 3:1-2

For this reason I, Paul, the prisoner of Christ Jesus for you Gentiles — 2 if indeed you have heard of the dispensation of the grace of God which was given to me for you. ...NKJV

Foundation

Before you begin this journey please note that this book was written from a Baptist doctrinal view point. However, also note that this information is helpful for all believers, no matter the denomination in which you practice your faith. If we hold dear the Holy Writ of God, we can still reason with one another to grow in the grace and knowledge of God.

Several tools were used to aid in this journey:

1. <u>Hermeneutics</u>: The science of interpretation, especially as it relates to the Scriptures and Biblical exegesis. *(See Appendix A, pg. 147)*

    a. For example, in summarizing a book of the Bible, or reading a passage of Scripture; utilization of this simplified format to begin the process of rightly dividing the Word of Truth for Bible scholars.

Book Summary Table	
(Example)	
Name of Book:	*What is the name of the book?*
Author:	*Who did the Holy Spirit use to write the book?*
Initially addressed to:	*To whom was it written?*
Date:	*Possible dates/timeframe that the book was written?*
Type of Book:	*For example, is the book history, prophecy, or poetry, etc.?*

Dispensation:	*In which dispensation is the book found within the Canon?*
Background	*What is taking place during this time?*
Book Theme:	*What is the over-arching theme of the book?*
Primary Application:	*These principles should be applied most importantly to whom?*
Secondary Application:	*These principles should be applied secondarily to whom?*
Key Passage(s)	*Highlighted Scripture to commit to memory*

    b. As outlined in J. Edwin Hartill's, book, <u>Principles of Biblical Hermeneutics</u>, there are 23 tenents or principles of Biblical hermeneutics. Hartill has done an outstanding job in delineating this masterful tool. Not only has he explained the principles; he has also provided helpful examples. Once learned and practiced, Bible students will have gained a better understanding of this science to properly divide and interpret Scripture. (See Appendix A, pg. 147)

2. <u>Dispensations</u>: Are the way in which God chooses to deal with man during a particular period of time to show man that he cannot be made righteous apart from Him. The Bible is divided into 7 dispensations or ages. God requires blood and faith in each for reconciliation. (See Appendix B, pg. 159):

    a. INNOCENCE

      b. CONSCIENCE
      c. HUMAN GOVERNMENT
      d. PROMISE
      e. LAW
      f. CHURCH or GRACE

> 7 years of
> TRIBULATION (3.5
> years of Tribulation
> and 3.5 years of the
> GREAT
> TRIBULATION)

      g. THE MILLENNIAL KINGDOM

(Note: Some dispensationalists count the Tribulation period as an additional dispensation; instead of 7, it would be 8. Hartill lists 8 and not 7). (See Appendix B, page 159).

3. <u>Reference books</u>: Various Bibles, Strong's Concordance, Vine's Dictionary, and additional lexicons.

4. <u>Additional references:</u> From fellow Theologians' books, lectures, papers, sites, and Biblical computer applications (Biblesoft's PC Study Bible 4 and The MacArthur Lifeworks Library/Libronix Digital Library System).

2 Ptr 1:20-21

… knowing this first, that no prophecy of Scripture is of any private interpretation, 21 for prophecy never came by the will of man, but holy men of God spoke as they were moved by the Holy Spirit. NKJV

Introduction

Baptists believe in the inerrancy of Scripture and that it has the highest authority over all else. *All Scripture is given by inspiration of God* (II Tim 3:16, NKJV). Baptists not only believe that Scripture has authority, but also has been clearly written for our understanding and that it is necessary for our salvation and living: *All Scripture is profitable for doctrine, for reproof, for correction, for instruction in righteousness, 17 that the man of God may be complete, thoroughly equipped for every good work* (II Tim 3:16b-17, NKJV). Even though all of the things of the Godhead (God the Father, God the Son (Jesus), and God the Holy Spirit) are not housed in the Bible, it is sufficient for us to know all the things God wanted us to know so that we may believe and grow and have a personal relationship with Him.

In reviewing Christian Theology, Baptist doctrine is usually proponents of systematic Theology. Systematic Theology as described by Wayne Grudem, is any study that answers the question, "What does the <u>whole</u> Bible teach us today about any given topic."[1] This systematic approach to Scripture is usually divided into nine divisions:

1. BIBLIOLOGY (DOCTRINE OF SCRIPTURES)
    from the Greek word: **βίβλος** (**biblŏs**, *bib´-los)*

2. THEOLOGY PROPER (DOCTRINE OF GOD THE FATHER) *from the Greek word:* **θεός** (**Thĕŏs**, *Theh´-os)*

3. CHRISTOLOGY (DOCTRINE OF JESUS CHRIST THE SON) *from the Greek word:* **Χριστός (Christŏs,** Khristos*)*

4. PNEUMATOLOGY (DOCTRINE OF THE HOLY SPIRIT) *from the Greek word:* **πνεῦμα (pnĕuma,** pnyoo´-mah*)note: Holy Spirit is shown as "Holy or Holy One" (**Hagiŏs,** Hag´-ee-os). Pnuema is breath*

5. ANGELOLOGY (DOCTRINE OF ANGELS) *from the Greek word:* **ἄγγελος (aggĕlŏs,** ang´-el-os*)*

6. ANTHROPOLOGY (DOCTRINE OF MAN) *from the Greek word:* **ἄνθρωπος (anthrōpŏs,** anth´-ro-pos)*

7. SOTERIOLOGY (DOCTRINE OF SALVATION AND JUSTIFICATION) *from the Greek word:* **σωτήρ, σωτηρία (sōtēr,** so-tare*)*

8. ECCESIOLOGY (DOCTRINE OF THE CHURCH) *from the Greek word:* **ἐκκλησία (ĕkklēsia,** ek-klay-see´-ah*)*

9. ESCHATOLOGY (DOCTRINE OF LAST THINGS OR END TIMES) *from the Greek word:* **ἔσχατος (ĕschatōs,** es-khat´-oce*)*

These divisions are easily recognizable within the 1833 New Hampshire Declaration of Faith in which we hold dear. This declaration of faith seems to be the layman's attempt to further breakdown Theological truths for easier understanding. *(See Appendix C, pg. 169)* [2]

PART 1

The Journey Begins

If a non-believer or new Christian only had access to one book of the Bible, which book should it be? I would have to suggest Romans. Romans provide the most ideal snapshot of God's glory and His sovereignty and man's deplorable nature. This book continues to display the wonderful works of God through each of the Persons of the Godhead. The Apostle Paul penned these brilliant teachings (doctrines) via the power of the Holy Spirit, during the 6th dispensation, *"The Church Age."* Supporting Scriptures throughout the Holy Writ strengthens this "access to only one book" scenario.

By the time we complete this leg of the journey; we will have a better understanding of why it is so important to know if our salvation is secure, is election a real thing, and how does free will operate within God's programming.

Utilizing simplified hermeneutics as an example, a Romans'
summary table could look like this:

Book Summary Table
(Romans' Example)

Name of Book:	*ROMANS*
Author:	*Paul, the apostle to the Gentile*
Initially addressed to:	*Gentiles*
Date:	*Likely A.D. 56-58*
Type of Book:	*Epistle*
Dispensation:	*The 6th dispensation – Church/Grace*
Background	*Paul was fulfilling his mission by sharing the Gospel with the Gentiles. Through his mission work, several congregations (churches) were formed. Paul had not been able to visit Rome as of yet, so he wrote a letter instead. By the time Paul finally made it to Rome, he was a prisoner.*
Book Theme:	*God's righteousness; there is nothing man can do to merit God's righteousness. All of man's righteousnesses are filthy to Him.*
Primary Application:	*Gentile believers; written to believers in Rome*
Secondary Application:	*Jewish believers acknowledge, learn, then do!*
Key Passage(s)	***Rom 1:16*** *For I am not ashamed of the gospel of Christ, for it is the power of God to salvation for everyone who believes, for the Jew first and also for the Greek.*
	Rom 3:9-12 *What then? Are we better than they? Not at all. For we have previously charged both Jews and Greeks that they are all under sin. As it is written: "There is none righteous, no, not one; There is none who understands; There is none who seeks after God.*

They have all turned aside;
They have together become unprofitable;
There is none who does good, no, not one."

Rom 3:23
For all have sinned and fall short of the
glory of God.

Rom 5:8
But God demonstrates his own love for us
in this: while we were still sinners, Christ
died for us.

Rom 6:23
For the wages of sin is death, but the gift
of God is eternal life in Christ Jesus our
Lord.

Rom 8:9
You however, are controlled not by the
sinful nature, but by the Spirit, if the
Spirit of God lives in you. And if anyone
does not have the Spirit of Christ, he does
not belong to Christ.

Rom 8:28-30
And we know that all things work
together for good to those who love God,
to those who are the called according to
His purpose. For whom He foreknew, He
also predestined to be conformed to the
image of His Son, that He might be the
firstborn among many brethren.
Moreover whom He predestined, these He
also called; whom He called, these He also
justified; and whom He justified, these He
also glorified.

Rom 8:37-39
Yet in all these things we are more than
conquerors through Him who loved us.
For I am persuaded that neither death nor
life, nor angels nor principalities nor

> powers, nor things present nor things to come, nor height nor depth, nor any other created thing, shall be able to separate us from the love of God which is in Christ Jesus our Lord.
>
> **Rom 10:9-13**
> . . .that if you confess with your mouth the Lord Jesus and believe in your heart that God has raised Him from the dead, you will be saved. For with the heart one believes unto righteousness, and with the mouth confession is made unto salvation. For the Scripture says, "Whoever believes on Him will not be put to shame." For there is no distinction between Jew and Greek, for the same Lord over all is rich to all who call upon Him. For "whoever calls on the name of the LORD shall be saved."
>
> **Rom 12:1-2**
> I beseech you therefore, brethren, by the mercies of God, that you present your bodies a living sacrifice, holy, acceptable to God, which is your reasonable service. And do not be conformed to this world, but be transformed by the renewing of your mind, that you may prove what is that good and acceptable and perfect will of God.

After perusing the summary table, we can begin to see the context of the book. We learn that Paul is the author and the approximate time of when it was written. The overall arching theme is about God's righteousness and man's unworthiness. Several key verses have been shared to support this theme. As we begin to delve deeper into the details of Romans, it is more helpful to divide the book into 3 distinct sections:

- DOCTRINAL (Chapters 1-8)
- DISPENSATIONAL (Chapters 9-11)
- DUTY (Chapters 12-16)

The first eight chapters are foundational teachings and are speaking to the Body of Christ as a whole (Jews and Gentiles). Paul's teachings focus on how God has been revealing Himself to man; how deplorable man is; and why we need a Savior. The next three chapters are considered dispensational focusing on how God chose Israel to tell the world about Him and His sovereignty, including the doctrine of *Election*.

The final five chapters build and culminate what was taught in the previous chapters. The commandment presented is: *Now that we know these truths, we now have the duty to obey and serve Him.* The whole duty of man is to obey God and keep His commandments *(Ecc 12:13)*. Our call to action is, to renew our minds daily and commit ourselves to Him *(Rom 12:1-2)*; to the One who owns everything; to whom we owe our allegiance, our lives *(Rom, 11:36, Col 1:9-18)*. The major themes gleaned throughout these chapter divisions will deepen our insights regarding doctrinal truths and help us to reason with one another more repletely through the power of the Holy Spirit.

Rom 1:20

For since the creation of the world His invisible attributes are clearly seen, being understood by the things that are made, even His eternal power and Godhead, so that they are without excuse ... NKJV

Chapter 1

Can Man Know God

Have you ever asked these questions, "Does God really exist?" or "Can man really know God?" The Scriptures answer, "Yes, God really exists; and yes, man can really know God." These magnificent declarations are shared, without a shadow of a doubt, that there is a God and we can know Him, because in *Romans (Rom) 1:19-20*, states:

> *...because what may be known of God is manifest in them, for God has shown it to them. For since the creation of the world His invisible attributes are clearly seen, being understood by the things that are made, even His eternal power and Godhead, so that they are without excuse... (NKJV)*

God is clear, even if for some reason a person may not have heard the Gospel (the Good News, *Greek (Gr):* εὐαγγέλιον [*euaggelion* /yoo·ang·**ghel**·ee·on/]), God has placed it in man to know through His creation that He exists. God's invisible attributes are seen within nature. In every tree, animal, and blade of grass, God has signed His masterpiece. *Genesis (Gen) 1:1* tells us that He spoke and things came into being from nothing. One must marvel at this because we as humans can't just walk outside and say, "tree be" and one grows. We have to use some type of starter kit that God has provided (example: seeds). *Psalm (Ps) 104* is further testimony that the "*earth is full of Your possessions*" and *I Corinthians (Cor) 10:26* testifies to that point as well. The Word even tells us in *Ps 19:1-4* that the heavens declare His work:

> *The heavens declare the glory of God;*
> *And the firmament shows His handiwork.*
> *Day unto day utters speech,*
> *And night unto night reveals knowledge.*
> *There is no speech nor language*
> *Where their voice is not heard.*
> *Their line has gone out through all the earth,*
> *And their words to the end of the world. (NKJV)*

But if man never picked up the Word of God to see it for himself, he would still be without excuse. Once again, man can try and say that they may have never heard the Gospel, but the sky, stars, sun, and moon are everywhere throughout the world and man did not place them there. Man can't even remove them. Furthermore, man with all of his great inventions still can't make rain fall from the sky on demand. So if "*the earth is the Lord's and the fullness thereof,*" (*I Cor 10:26*) everything and everyone belongs to Him. God is not only the creator of life, but the sustainer of life. Man can't even decide on which continent he is going to be born because God also predetermines this tidbit *(Acts 17:26-28)*.

Chapter 2

The Depravity of Man

Romans 1:24-32
24 Therefore God also gave them up to uncleanness, in the lusts of their hearts, to dishonor their bodies among themselves, 25 who exchanged the truth of God for the lie, and worshiped and served the creature rather than the Creator, who is blessed forever. Amen.

26 For this reason God gave them up to vile passions. For even their women exchanged the natural use for what is against nature. 27 Likewise also the men, leaving the natural use of the woman, burned in their lust for one another, men with men committing what is shameful, and receiving in themselves the penalty of their error which was due.

28 And even as they did not like to retain God in their knowledge, God gave them over to a debased mind, to do those things which are not fitting; 29 being filled with all unrighteousness, sexual immorality, wickedness, covetousness, maliciousness; full of envy, murder, strife, deceit, evil-mindedness; they are whisperers, 30 backbiters, haters of God, violent, proud, boasters, inventors of evil things, disobedient to parents, 31 undiscerning, untrustworthy, unloving, unforgiving, unmerciful; 32 who, knowing the righteous judgment of God, that those who practice such things are deserving of death, not only do the same but also approve of those who practice them. (NKJV)

Unbelievers refused to glorify God as the one and only true God, therefore, He left them to themselves. And since man already has a corrupt nature because of sin, their thoughts continued to spiral downward because their consciences are seared *(I Timothy (Tim) 4:2)*. So these unbelievers dishonored their bodies, and started believing the lie that it is okay to mix the sexes. God had said, let there be man and woman, so that they can procreate. The unbelieving creature said, "No! God has it wrong!" One man says "I was created to be with a man;" then an unbelieving woman says, "God has it wrong; I was born to be with a woman." So God allowed them to themselves to see how far down they would spiral and these debase unbelievers continued spiraling out of control and went against God's design and did disgusting things with the same sex.

The more these sin-sick/spiritually dead creatures refused to turn to God, the more they moved themselves from being right with Him and plunged head first into deeper sexual acts that continued to fall away from God's design. God created man and woman to populate the earth. Genesis (Gen) 1:27-28 says, *"So God created man in His own image; in the image of God He created him; male and female He created them. 28 Then God blessed them, and God said to them, 'Be fruitful and multiply.'"* God has placed the inner workings of procreation in each sex in order for this to occur. Two men cannot keep this commandment, nor can two women. For the Word of the Lord says in *Proverbs (Prov) 3:32, "For the perverse person is an abomination to the LORD."* All throughout God's Word, in the Old Testament and New Testament alike, God says that males should not lie with other men like they lie with women (*Leviticus (Lev) 18:22, Lev 20:13, I Cor 6:9, and I Tim 1:9-10*).

Their whole minds and beings were engrossed in lewd behavior. These sad creatures were haters of God and Godly things, and began to think of new ways in which to express their evil. God is clear, to do so is not just a sin, but is a detestation. God hates sin, but an abomination is a sin in which He hates emphatically. The wages of sin is still death, no matter how you slice it. Practicing homosexuals/lesbians will not make it into the Kingdom of Heaven. But there is hope for a person who has practiced this lifestyle and would like to be delivered. God can cure <u>all sin</u>. One just has to turn to Him and ask to be washed in the blood. God's sanctifying power will remove this sin taste from us. *I John (Jn) 1:9* is clear, that if we confess our sins, God will cleanse us from all unrighteousness. God is holy, and in turn, those who serve Him must be set apart for service. These lewd behaviors are all out of the plan for righteous living and sin must be punished *(Rom 3:23)*.

Rom 3:10-11

As it is written:
"There is none righteous,
no, not one;
11 There is none who
understands;
There is none who seeks
after God. NKJV

Chapter 3

The Moral-Good Man

In the second chapter of Romans, the moralist, religionist, or legalist man is explained. He is one who believes he can merit heaven because he is inherently good. This person believes that because God saw some good in him, he can go to heaven because of this *"good"* that God saw in him. A moralist believes that he will escape judgment, and that God is too good of a God to send people to hell. And justifying himself with these dubious thoughts hardens his heart against God's truth about judgment.

This good man is already judged for his conduct because he is built up with spiritual pride. And the very thing that he thinks he doesn't do, he does, and so his own actions condemn him. The principles of God's judgment are outlined in *Romans 2:2-16:*

1. According to truth *2:2*
2. According to deeds, *2:6*
3. According to no partiality, *2:11*
    a. Since Christ who knows the heart is judge
    b. They are in accord with Paul's Gospel

Man is not "basically good" *(Psalms (Ps) 14:3, Ps 53:3)*. Because of Adam's sin, mankind has been plunged into darkness *(Rom 5:12)* and needs a Reconciler to bring us back into the light. The moralist is blind to the fact that he cannot save himself. Biblical history has shown us this flaw in Adam and Eve. They believed the serpent's lie; that once they ate of the fruit of the Knowledge of Good and Evil, they would be like God. But as usual, satan did not tell them the entire story. It was true indeed that Adam and Eve would know the difference between good and evil, but the rest of the story remained untold to them. This is the part that was left out: just because they had this knowledge, they would not have the ability to choose good over evil. Man's conscience has been seared ever since *(I Tim 4:2)*, so their perspective is warped. They have exchanged the truth for a lie, and therefore will suffer the consequences of their actions. Whatever man thinks is good enough to merit heaven, will always miss the mark *(Gr:* ἁμαρτία *[hamartia /ham·ar·***tee***·ah/])*.

In Romans 2:7, the Scriptures mention deeds or good works and eternal life in the same sentence. Many Theologians teach that this means one must work to be saved or stay saved. But Theologians who teach this doctrine are in error. For God is clear on what we must do to be saved in this dispensation.

In every dispensation God requires blood and faith; and in this Age of Grace (Church Age) God has not changed the requirement. The blood given in this age belongs to Jesus. God tells us that Jesus is the free gift that has been given for our sins *(Rom 5:8)*.

God is emphatic that it is not about works, but about faith *(Eph 2:8-9)*. Our requirement is to believe that Jesus is who He says He is, *(Jn 14:2)*. In *I Corinthians 15:3-4*, the Bible tells us what the *Good News* is: Jesus' death, burial and resurrection. Once we believe on the finished work of Christ, His free gift to us, then we are assured of eternal life. *John 17:3-4* says, *"And this is eternal life, that they may know You, the only true God, and Jesus Christ whom You have sent."* (NKJV) Our requirement is to believe as stated in *Romans 10: 9-10*, *"That if thou shalt confess with thy mouth the Lord Jesus, and shalt believe in thine heart that God hath raised him from the dead, thou shalt be saved. For with the heart man believeth unto righteousness; and with the mouth confession is made unto salvation."* (KJV)

However, because of man's pride, he always tries to take God out of the equation, and build himself up to try and merit heaven. Theologians who take this Scripture out of context are guilty of doing this same thing. The Bible always affirms itself because it is the inerrant Word of God. Looking at *Ephesians 2:10* illuminates this verse so that we see, once we are in Christ Jesus and the Holy Spirit lives in us, we have been crafted to do good works. We can only do *"good works"* once we've become saved, not before. God is clear; all of our righteousnesses are as filthy rags *(Is 64:6)*. Man cannot merit salvation in what he does as far as deeds are concerned.

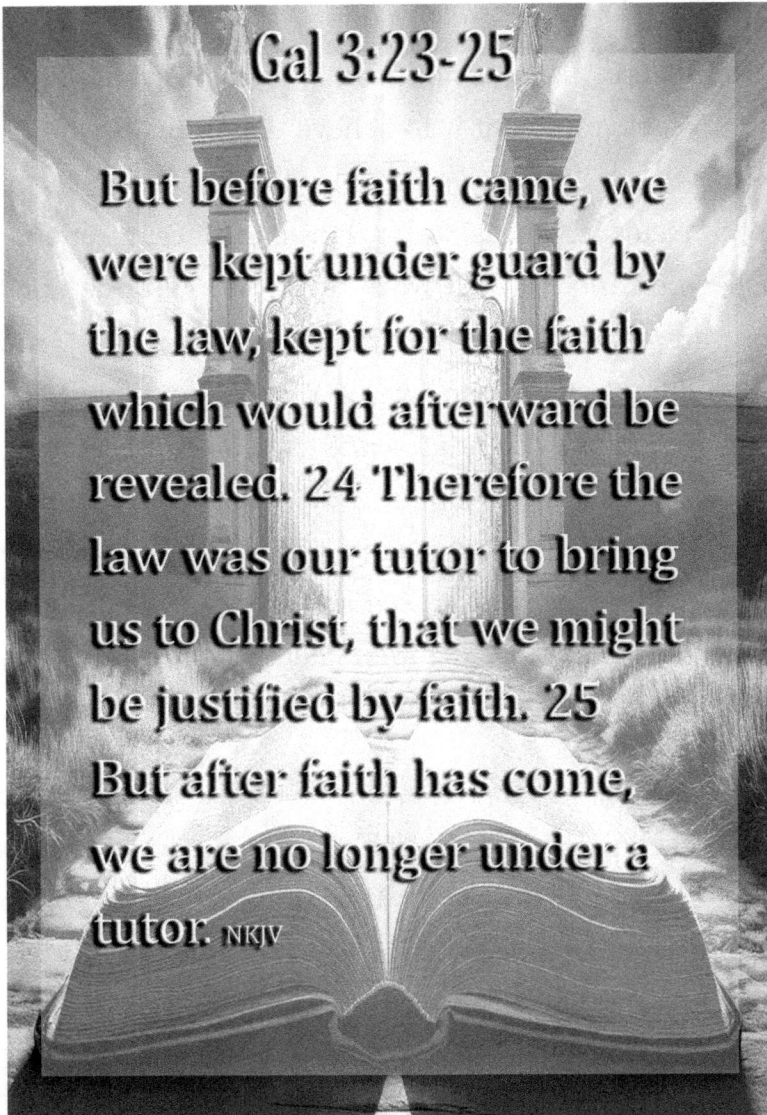

Gal 3:23-25

But before faith came, we were kept under guard by the law, kept for the faith which would afterward be revealed. 24 Therefore the law was our tutor to bring us to Christ, that we might be justified by faith. 25 But after faith has come, we are no longer under a tutor. NKJV

Chapter 4

The Law Abiding Man

Unbelief of the Jews or Gentiles does not make the faith of God without effect. The faith of God and His Word are one. The Scripture says, *"let God be true, but every man a liar" (Rom 3:4 KJV)*. *"God is not a man that He should lie" (Num 23:19)*. Religionists believe that since they have the Law and their rituals; that this is all they need to be saved. But the Law has no saving power, and was only created to show man his wrong; it was their elementary schoolmaster pointing them to Christ *(Gal 3:24)*.

When man holds up his works as an entry fee into Heaven, God's Words hold true and every man is proven to be a liar. <u>Only faith plus nothing</u> merits Heaven. It is Christ's finished work on the cross that is the entry fee. In Matthew the 23rd chapter, Jesus shares the woes of these religious hypocrites that trust more in the created processes than the Creator. Jesus warns them of their eminent doom for misplacing their trust in their own works and not in Him *(I Peter (Ptr) 1:18-19, I Tim 2:5, Jn 3:3)*.

Man's works are vile, and the religious man continues to prove God's Words are true. God is a faithful God, and He is His Word. What He says must be accomplished. God says that sin must be punished, and unbelief will send you to hell. His Word will not return void, and this is exactly what will occur to unbelievers. The religious man will not be spared because of his unbelief *(Is 55:11, Rom 11:19-21)*.

The religious man acknowledges the Law and meditates on it day and night, and yet is blinded to the truth. The very thing that they hold dear has condemned them. God's testimony was given to them first (the Jews) so they could go and tell the whole world about Him. Instead they were puffed up with spiritual pride because God's Word had been given to them. They may have been keepers of His Word, but they were not believers and followers of His Holy Mandates. For God said in *Ezekiel 18:20 "The soul that sinneth, it shall die." (KJV)*

Dr. Jimmy Hayes shares fourteen charges that have been laid out against the religious man in *Romans 3:10-18* for self-righteousness:

1. There is none righteous, no, not one

Because of one man's sin (Adam), we all inherited a sin nature *(Rom 5:12)*. *Psalms 51:55* says, *"Behold, I was shapen in iniquity; and in sin did my mother conceive me."* Because Adam is our corporate head, <u>all</u> have missed the mark (ἁμαρτία / *hamartia*) of God's requirements *(Rom 3:23)* for right standing with Him.

2. There is none who understands

Our sinful minds are warped *(I Tim 4:2)*. And if God does not reach over into the realm of darkness and pluck us out, we would continue to be blind to the fact that we need a Savior. In John 16:8-11, we see the ministries of the Holy Spirit: *"And when he is come, he will reprove the world of sin, and of righteousness, and of judgment: Of sin, because they believe not on me; Of righteousness, because I go to my Father, and ye see me no more; Of judgment, because the prince of this world is judged" (KJV)*. The Holy Spirit is the one who convinces us that we are sinners and need to be saved. God tells us that the beginning of knowledge and understanding begins with Him *(Ps 111:10, Prov 1:7, Prov 9:10.)* Unless God illuminates our hearts and mind, man will never understand.

3. There is none who seek after God

Proverbs 1:7 tells us that fools or the wicked don't seek after God, and only a fool says in his heart that God does not exist; and fools care not to know the truth *(Ps 14:1, Ps 10: 4, Prov 18:2, Rom 3:11)*.

4. They are all gone out of the way

Jesus is the way, the truth, and the life *(Jn 14:6)*; no one can get to the Father unless they go through Him. But man has gone out of his way to accept his own righteousness *(Prov 14:12, 16:25)* which will ultimately lead to death. As previously discussed in *Romans 1:18-32*; God gave ignorant man over to their own consciences and they continued to spiral downward until they were swimming in lies and corruption.

5. They are together become unprofitable

Building on the previous verses, man continued to seethe disgusting things. Because they have been given over to complete corruptibleness, they are utterly useless *(all previous verses)*.

6. There is none that doeth good, no, not one

Man, being a slave to sin, can only do its bidding until there is an intervention; there is nothing good in him *(Ps 14:1, Prov 15:9, Prov 21:8)*. So man is in error when statements are made like, "he is a good man;" because inherently, no one is good, except Christ; He is the Good Shepherd, the Holy One of Israel *(II Chronicles (Chron) 6:14, Jn 10:11, 14)*.

7. Their throat is an open sepulcher

Man's very being is rotten, and stinks as if it is an open grave. The smell is horrendous and the stench unapproachable; his bones and mouth are full of sin *(Job 20:11-12)*.

8. With their tongues they have used deceit

Psalms 10:7 states that the wicked man's mouth if full of cursing, deceit and oppression. Their mouths are full of evil and their tongues are framed in deceit *(Ps 50:19-20)*.

9. The poison of Asps is under their lips

From man's inner most being is fowl like deadly snakes *(Job 20:14)* and the tongue defiles the entire body *(James 3:6)*.

10. Whose mouth is full of cursing and bitterness

Their mouths are full of lies and cursing spewing from their pride. The bitterness of their disposition causes trouble and poisons their surroundings and it spreads like a cancer *(Ps 10:7, Ps 59:12, Acts 8:23, Heb 12:15)*.

11. Their feet are swift to shed blood

These keepers of the Law (not doers, just holders) are full of evil *(Rom 1:29)*. Their ultimate murderous act was the crucifixion of Jesus Christ *(Luke 22, 23:21)*. They were quick to persecute Jesus and those of "The Way" *(Acts 22:4)* in order to maintain their place of authority—maintaining their own self-righteousness as an entrance fee into heaven so that they can boast *(Ps 94:4)*.

12. Destruction and misery are in their ways

Because of their haughty spirit and pridefullness, their road leads to destruction *(Prov 16:18)*. Because no good is found in them, they are incapable of doing good and there is no deliverance from wickedness *(Ecc 8:6-8)*.

13. The way of peace have they not known

To have Christ is to have peace with God *(Rom 5:1)*. These evil doers can't know peace because they don't know the mediator, Jesus Christ, who bridges the Gap between God and man. They can't experience the peace of God *(Phil 4:7)* until they have peace with God. One has to be saved first, before he can receive the continual cleansing of Jesus Christ (Salvation first, then Sanctification); *first things first!*

14. There is no fear of God before their eyes

God will not be mocked, whatever man sows he will reap *(Gal 6:7)*. The fear of the Lord is the beginning of wisdom. Fools despise wisdom *(Ps 111:10, Prov 9:10)* because they have said in their heart that God does not exist *(Ps 14: 1)*. Fools will be without excuse on Judgment Day *(Heb 9:27)*. These foolish men have convinced themselves that their own righteousness can merit heaven. But God said that this is not so, for all of their righteousnesses are as filthy rags *(Isaiah (Isa) 64:6)*.

Scripture is so very clear, and this has become a "drop the mic" moment. This law-abiding man has still missed the mark. All that he has done and hopes to do in keeping the Law has already failed; and again, there will be no excuse for him because he refused to believe God's Words. He'd rather count on his own "self-righteousnesses," instead of the righteousness of God!

Chapter 5

Propitiation

Propitiation in Romans 3:25 refers to God's redemptive plan for man through Jesus Christ. A secular dictionary offers a definition while a spiritual dictionary offers another:

> **Secular**: the act of gaining or regaining the favor or goodwill of someone or something: the act of <u>propitiating</u>; **Appeasement**

> **Spiritual:** the act of atoning for sin or wrongdoing (especially appeasing a deity)
> **-Atonement, Expiation**
> **-Redemption, Salvation** – (Theology) the act of delivering from sin or saving from evil
> **-Amends, Reparation** – something done or paid in expiation of a wrong; "how can I make amends"

Several synonyms for propitiation are recorded. Reconciliation and payment are the ones that will be used for our examples.

Jesus was the payment for our sins; because of His finished work, God brought us back, or reconciled us back unto Himself. During the Dispensation of the Law (the 5th dispensation), the Levitical Priesthood was in order. Each year, the High Priest had to go into the Holy of Holies and place the blood of the sacrificial animal on the mercy seat. This act would cover the sins of the Jewish people for one year. Each year, a scapegoat had to be led far out of the camp of the meeting. Yet each year, these same acts had to be repeated—year after year while the dispensation of the Law lasted. Unfortunately, this required ritual never permanently removed their sins, only covered them.

But behold, God was going to do a new thing. John the Baptist said, *"Behold, the Lamb of God, who takes away the sins of the world" (Jn 1:29)*. God's redemptive plan for man, allowed a High Priest who would come, and not only be the Sacrificer, but also the Sacrifice, and be our High Priest forever *(Heb 4)*. Jesus, our slain goat as well as our scapegoat bought us back with a price that did more than just cover or atone for the sins of the people; He took them away forever--*as far as the East is from the West (Ps 103:12)*. In *I John 2:2; 4:10*, Christ is called the "propitiation for our sins." Here, the *Greek* word is used here is ἱλασμός *(hilasmos)* meaning propitiation.

The mercy seat represents Christ, where God meets man and he is shown mercy. The <u>new thing</u> was the Cross of Christ; which now represents the public showing of what had previously taken place in private in the Holy of Holies. No longer just for the Jewish people, but for those *"whosoever will call upon Him" (Rom 10:9-13) (NKJV)*.

Because of Adam's sin, a sin nature was imparted to all mankind *(Rom 5:12)*. This sinful nature was brought about by deceit through the lust of the flesh, the lust of the eyes and the pride of life *(I Jn 2:16)*. This is the same formula satan used in the Garden of Eden, and still uses today to attack man. Man is so prideful, that at first, he doesn't think anything is wrong with him. Then the Holy Spirit convinces him that there is something wrong with him *(Jn 16:8)* and he needs a Savior. Man then goes about trying to save himself, but to no avail. God is clear in *His Word*, that the only way to Him is through His Son *(Jn 14:6)* and it is by His grace alone so that man will have no room for boasting *(Eph 2:8-9)*. Because of God's wonderful bookkeeping system called "imputation" which means "to reckon or charge to one's account;" *The Way* has been made to zero their account. A plan had been put in place where Adam's sin no longer had to be the ruling order. These three things occur during imputation:

1. Adam's sin on all of mankind *(Rom 5:12)*

2. Our sin on Jesus *(Isa 53, II Cor 5: 17-21)*

3. Jesus' Righteousness on us *(II Cor 5:21b)*

In order for man to receive the correction from the first imputation, he has to believe as Abram did in *Genesis 15:6* and boast in the Lord, not in his own righteousness which is a position of pride, and of his own works.

With God, it will always be about belief and not one's own religious behavior which speaks of works in ritual. God stayed Abraham's hand and provided a ram in the bush *(Gen 22:13)*. Israel was told to, *"stand still, and see the salvation of the Lord" (Ex 14:13)*. Even in these acts, God was demanding faith, not works as a savoring aroma. It takes God to please God *(Rom 11:36)*, therefore God has given each man a measure of faith that can be quickened when the Holy Spirit calls. Abraham's spiritual seed are the ones whose hearts have been circumcised.

The Hebrew writer's theme is *"a more excellent way"* and that way is by Grace; which is far better than the prophets, and better than the Law of Moses *(Heb 1:4)*. God's unmerited favor, in which He chose not to give us what we deserve--**mercy**, but instead, He chose to give us what we don't deserve--**grace**. The Law states, "If you do good then I will bless you." This is the conditional manner of the Law of Moses. Grace states, "I have blessed you, now do good." By doing good, it is the response of the blessing in which one has already received. God points out in *Romans 4:9-15* that belief always supersedes the Law; and believers are to respond as Abraham did, so our belief will place us into God's bookkeeping system.

Chapter 6

Benefits

Ps 103:1-2
Bless the LORD, O my soul;
And all that is within me, bless His holy name!
2 Bless the LORD, O my soul,
And forget not all His benefits (NKJV)

Several benefits are imparted to the believer once God has snatched him out of darkness and placed him into the marvelous Light. Let's review two scholars' presentations of these benefits, Dr. Jimmy Hayes, from Andersonville Theological Seminary and Dr. Lewis Sperry Chafer of Dallas Theological Seminary.

Dr. Hayes has noted 8 benefits of Salvation which are found in *Romans 5:1-11*:

1. **Peace** - The believer has peace with God. Through the blood of Christ, we have been reconciled back into the fold and no longer have to suffer the consequences of sin *(Rom 6:23)*. The believer is no longer God's adversary but a joint heir with Christ.

2. **Access to God in prayer** - Because of the Peace with God, the believer now has access to God in prayer. He hears us in His temple *(Ps 18:6)*. We are told to come boldly before His throne *(Heb 4:16)* and make our request unto Him *(Phil 4:6)*.

3. **Hope of the Glory of God** - *Titus 2:13* tells us that we have a hope--a definite expectation to see His marvelous glory. We have the blessed hope of seeing His face, because nothing can separate us from Him *(Rom 8:35)*.

4. **Triumph in trouble** - The believer has triumph in trouble because the Scripture tells us so. Romans 8:37 tells us that we are more than conquerors when we face trials. The Psalmists tells us that during our fiery periods, the Lord is our strength and refuge *(9:9, 27:5, 37:9, 46:1)*. God comforts us when we are troubled; *(II Cor 1:3-4)* even when we are pressed all about us, we are not destroyed *(II Cor 4:8-12)*. We are comforted knowing that even though our afflictions are great, the Lord delivers us from them all *(Ps 34:19)*.

5. **The Love of God** - Believers have the Love of God *(II Cor 13:14)* which has been poured out in our hearts *(Rom 5:5)*. The same love that compelled Christ to the cross is the same love we now possess. Because He first loved us while we were yet sinners *(Rom 5:8)*, we now have the

power through the Holy Spirit, to love as He has shown us.

6. **The Indwelling of the Holy Spirit** - Believers now have the Holy Spirit residing in them *(II Tim 1:14)*; our bodies are the temple of the Holy Spirit *(I Cor 6:19)*.

7. **Deliverance from wrath** - As Noah and his family were saved from the wrath of God during the flood *(Gen 6 & 7)*, so shall the Church be saved from the tribulation period *(I Thess 1:10, 5:9)*.

8. **Joy in God** – Believers are blessed with joy, unspeakable joy because we have been reconciled back unto the Father *(Job 33:26)*. There is none like our God!

Moreover, Dr. Lewis Sperry Chafer expresses the benefits of Salvation in his work "Systematic Theology," a more replete depiction of these riches of God's divine grace that the believer receives. I have re-phrased it as if a new employee is onboarding who needs to receive pertinent information regarding his company benefits. Keeping in mind that genre, let's explore ***"The Believers' Benefit Package!"*** *(Ps 68:19, 103:2, 116:12)*.

"The Believers' Benefit Package!"
(Ps 68:19, 103:2, 116:12)
33 riches of God's divine grace

1. In the Eternal Plan of God
2. Redeemed
3. Reconciled
4. Related to God thru Propitiation
5. Forgiven all Trespasses
6. Vitally Conjoined to Christ
7. Free from the Law
8. Children of God
9. Adopted
10. Acceptable to God by Jesus

    a. Made Righteous
    b. Sanctified Positionally
    c. Made Accepted in the Beloved
    d. Perfected Forever
    e. Made Meet (Together, Prepared)
11. Justified
12. Made nigh/near
13. Delivered from the Power of Darkness
14. Translated into the Kingdom of His Son
15. On the Rock
16. A Gift From God the Father to Christ
17. Circumcised in Christ
18. Partakers of the Holy & Royal Priesthood
19. A Chosen Generation
20. Heavenly Citizens
21. Of the Family & Household of God
22. In the Fellowship of the Saints
23. A Heavenly Association

    a. Partners with Christ in Life
    b. Partnership in Position
    c. Partners in Service
    d. Partners with Christ in Suffering
    e. Partners with Christ in Prayer
    f. Partners with Christ in Expectation
24. Having Access to God

    a. Access to His Grace
    b. Access to the Father
    c. Access is Reassuring

25. Within the much More Care
    of God
    a. Objects of His Love
    b. Objects of His Grace
    c. Object of Salvation
    d. Object of Safe Keeping
    e. Object of Service
    f. Object of Instruction
    g. Object of His Power
    h. Object of His
       Faithfulness
    i. Object of His Peace
    j. Object of His
       Consolation
    k. Object of His
       Intercession
26. His Inheritance
27. Inheritance of the Saints
28. Light on the Lord
29. Vitally United to the Trinity
30. Blessed with the First Fruits
    of the Spirit
31. Glorified
32. Complete in Him
33. Possessing Every Spiritual
    Blessing

Gal 4:4-5

But when the fullness of the time had come, God sent forth His Son, born of a woman, born under the law, 5 to redeem those who were under the law, that we might receive the adoption as sons. NKJV

Chapter 7

The Need for The Savior

Rom 5:12-15
Therefore, just as through one man sin entered the world, and
death through sin, and thus death spread to all men, because
all sinned — 13 For until the law sin was in the world, but sin is
not imputed when there is no law. 14 Nevertheless death
reigned from Adam to Moses, even over those who had not
sinned according to the likeness of the transgression of Adam,
who is a type of Him who was to come. 15 But the free gift is
not like the offense. For if by the one man's offense many died,
much more the grace of God and the gift by the grace of the one
Man, Jesus Christ, abounded to many. (NKJV)

Adam was the first man who came from red ground (hence the meaning of his name). In God's original plan, He gave Adam the job to tend to the Garden of Eden; name the animals and care for the gift God had crafted for him, Eve. It was also in God's original plan that when Eve bore children, she wouldn't experience any pain. God had given Adam and Eve free will, and He chose to test them to see if they would be obedient. God had given to them, wonderful, marvelous things which were almost too numerous to count. But God held one thing back from them to test their obedience—*The Tree of the Knowledge of Good and Evil* (*Gen 2:16-17*). Eve was deceived by the serpent, and Adam chose to partake of the fruit of that tree and failed the governmental test during the first dispensation. This act of disobedience plunged the entire world into chaos. The serpent was cursed to now travel on his belly and eat dirt, (*Gen 3:14*); a natural hatred was placed between the serpent and Eve as well as between the offspring of the serpent and Eve's offspring (*Gen 3:14*). The woman was cursed with painful childbearing and the desire to rule over her husband, but never being able to (*Gen 3:16*). The disobedience of this man caused the ground to be cursed and he was sentenced to work all the days of his life (*Gen 3:17-19*).

God told Adam in *Genesis 2:17* that if he ate of this tree that Adam would surely "die while dying" *(which is a more accurate interpretation in Hebrew).* Death simply means separation; and at that time, Adam and Eve died a spiritual death, while their physical bodies started decaying. Adam, in faith had named his wife Eve, the mother of all mankind (*Gen 3:20*). Therefore, God had set forth His redemptive plan because of His foreknowledge as stated in the first Messianic Promise in Scripture *(Gen 3:15,)* God honored Adam's faith. Even though God forgave Adam, Adam still had to deal with the consequences of his disobedience. Since we were all in Adam and Eve, the separated, fractured nature became a part of the Human Race, caused by this disobedient act. All men would come into the world with this fractured nature; missing God's mark; having to die because death is the culmination thereof. To clarify, Adam and Eve were the only ones who became sinners by sinning; the rest of us were born sinners.

God gave us a glimpse of His redemptive plan for man in *Genesis 3:15.* A body would be crafted for Christ *(Heb 10:5).* A Son would be given, and a child would be born *(Is 9:6).* Born of the Father so that the sin-nature would not travel down to Him; born of a virgin, so that Second Person of the Godhead, would bear the human experience. Christ, being the free gift that was given while we were yet sinners *(Rom 5:8)* was extended to us. Christ, the free gift, Who would freely choose to obey God unto death *(Phil 2:8)* showed us the way.

Even though Adam had a good life in the Garden and we were in him; those who believe and have been adopted have a much better place in Christ Jesus in Heaven, the Author and Finisher of our faith *(Heb 12:2);* our Justifier *(Rom 3:26);* our Hope of Glory *(Col 1:27)*! Where death now ruled and reigned, now Everlasting Life has victory over death, hell, and the grave *(I Cor 15:55).*

Eph 5:25-27

Husbands, love your wives, just as Christ also loved the church and gave Himself for her, 26 that He might sanctify and cleanse her with the washing of water by the word, 27 that He might present her to Himself a glorious church, not having spot or wrinkle or any such thing, but that she should be holy and without blemish. NKJV

Chapter 8

The Need for His Sanctification

Since we have been saved from the penalty of sin when we were justified; we have now been set apart for service. Sin no longer has power over us. At the moment of salvation, the Holy Spirit disconnected us from the old power supply and connected us to our new power source. Our new power supply-- the Holy Spirit--teaches us all things and teaches us how to choose good over evil; to choose God instead of serving the sinful nature. We as new creatures in Christ Jesus have two natures that reside in us. The two natures are constantly warring against one another (*Gal 5:17*) and we have to choose who is going to sit in the control seat: the Holy Spirit or the old man.

Before the Holy Spirit took up residency, man had no power over sin and it ruled without mercy (*Rom 5:20a, 21a*). But now, since the believer has been renewed with a right spirit within in him, he is no longer a slave to sin. The sin nature desires sinful things (*Gal 5:19-21*), and even though the flesh is never satisfied, it is constantly trying to be satiated. Unfortunately, the sinner is a slave to sin. Sin is his master and rules and reigns in the members of a sinner. Since the Holy Spirit now resides in the believer, the believer can stay connected to the new power supply who makes us want to choose good over evil (*Titus 2:11-13*). Because of the two warring natures within the believer, each moment the believer has to choose who shall sit in the seat of control, or which power supply will have dominance.

This dynamic is our sanctification process. Each day we walk with God, the easier it can become. Even though the trials may become greater, we possess the power to deal with them because the Holy Spirit teaches us all things; yea even the deep things of God (*I Cor 2:10*). Whichever power supply we choose, we become slaves to its authority--slaves of sin, or slaves of righteousness. If we walk according to the leading of the Holy Spirit, we won't succumb to the lust of the flesh (*Gal 5:16*). Believers have a choice, and when we choose not to listen to the Holy Spirit, we grieve Him (*Eph 4:30*).

Furthermore, if we are dead to sin, sin no longer has power over us. A dead body can't do sinful things. It is when we choose to disconnect from the Holy Spirit and re-connect the old power supply that we allow the old nature to rule at that moment (*Rom 6:4*). This is the constant battle for the two-natured believer. Paul addresses this struggle in depth in *Romans 7* as a "moment by moment" battle.

Chapter 9

The New Way

In chapter six of *Romans*, Paul shares with us the new way, or mechanism put in place, which is better than the old system of the law. This new way is Grace. He continues his discussion of how the new way works, and the struggles that are indeed prevalent in the following types of men. Three kinds of men are discussed in *Romans 7:1-25*, the Spiritual Man, the Natural Man, and the Carnal Man.

Paul shares with us in *verses 1-6* the Spiritual Man who is now plugged into the new power source and receiving energy for sustaining power. The old man has died to sin; hence the Law no longer has any power over him. The Law was in affect when the old man ruled, but since he has been crucified with Christ he has been promoted into new life (*Rom 6:6, Gal 2:20*). Now, because the Holy Spirit lives in him, he has the ability to choose good over evil--the new power source is the revitalizing authority that makes this possible (*I Cor 2:12-13*). The Spiritual Man is learning more and more how to yield to the Spirit as to not grieve the Spirit. Now this new creature, "The Spiritual Man," can walk in *The Way* of the Lord.

Verses 7-13 reveal the Natural Man who is still alive to sin, and therefore the Law condemns him already. The Law was given to expose sin that had been previously camouflaged. The Natural Man cannot understand spiritual things because he is spiritually dead (I *Cor 2:14*). Corpses don't need food, and can't enjoy the great taste of the Lord. The Law highlights sin and therefore death. It was never meant to save (*Gal 3:23-25*).

The Carnal Man is the last man that Paul discusses in *verses 14-25*. This man is a saved man, meaning he has been saved from the penalty of sin, but still chooses to be under the power of sin. Even though the mechanism has been put into place where he can access the new power supply, this babe in Christ is constantly disconnecting from the real, true, and good Power source and reconnecting to the damaged, crude, old, disgusting one. Carnal Christians don't want to move from their first state of salvation and move forward toward the deeper things of God. Essentially babes in Christ want to stay on milk instead of being weaned off of it to enjoy food with greater sustenance (*I Cor 3:1-3*).

Sin is the root cause of all behavioral problems in man. Christ is the only solution and His new power source has to be implanted. Even though the battle continues between the two natures while still in the earthly body; the believer will be saved one day, not just from the penalty and power, but eventually from the very presence of sin. God will create glorified bodies for believers crafted for eternity (*I Cor 15:52, I Ptr 1:23*).

Ps 103: 1-4

Bless the LORD, O my soul; And all that is within me, bless His holy name! 2 Bless the LORD, O my soul, And forget not all His benefits: 3 Who forgives all your iniquities, Who heals all your diseases, 4 Who redeems your life from destruction, Who crowns you with lovingkindness and tender mercies. … NKJV

Chapter 10

No Condemnation, No Separation

Romans the 8th chapter begins with no <u>condemnation</u> and ends with no <u>separation</u>. Once we are in Christ Jesus, we are no longer judged for our sins (condemned); which the penalty is death. Nor can we be disconnected from Him (separated); nothing or no one can snatch us out of His hands. Since we have become a part of Him, we are like Him, children of the Most High! Paul quotes *II Samuel 7:14* in his second letter to the Corinthians (*II Cor 6:18*) that once God separates us out we become His sons and daughters. *Romans 8:16* tells us that the Holy Spirit bears witness with our spirit of this adoption transaction, that we are God's children. The *17th verse* solidifies the adoption and moves from just children, to actual heirs. Believers get to partake in the riches of God, not just in name only, but everything which God has to offer also belongs to us. The acronym **RIBS**, illustrates the activities that take place the moment we believe on the death, burial, and resurrection of Christ:

R REGENERATED
Tit 3:5-regeneration – spiritual rebirth
Eph 2:1 – quickened ...re-animate conjointly
Eph 2:5-made alive together with Christ
Col 2:13-made alive together with Him
1 Pu 3:18-make alive, give life, revitalize

I INDWELT
Acts 2:4-filled with the Holy Spirit
1 Cor 6:19-Holy Spirit who is in you
II Tim 1:4-Holy Spirit dwells in you
Rom 8:11- Holy Spirit dwells in you

B BAPTIZED
1 Cor 12:13-baptized into one body

S SEALED
EPH 1:13-sealed, stamped, secured, and
preserved with the Holy Spirit of promise

The **RIBS** acronym could be tweaked to become either **RIBAS** or **RIBSA** to include adopted. *I John 3:9* tells us that once we've been born of Him, His seed remains within us. We are His now and forevermore. Nothing can separate us nor condemn us. Jesus cannot sin and His shed blood reconnects us back to God.

When Adam sinned in Genesis, he not only plunged the human race into sin, but all creation. Because of sin, the ground would be cursed and man would have to till the hard soil and deal with animals turning on him that he used to dominate *(Gen 3:17-21)*. All of creation is in an upheaval waiting for Christ to return *(Rom 8:18-22)*. All of creation is moaning and groaning hence the reason for earthquakes, pestilences, hurricanes; tornadoes, and floods. The earth is acting like it is in labor, trying to get rid of the sin that has been placed upon it.

Enmity was placed between man and animals; and animals and other animals. Wolves and children can't play together, nor can most beasts of the fields. This war that goes on is a result of Adam's disobedience. All of creation is awaiting the peace that only God can give. When Christ comes again, that animosity will no longer exist *(Isa 11:6-8)*.

Isa 29:16

Surely you have things turned around! Shall the potter be esteemed as the clay; For shall the thing made say of him who made it, "He did not make me"? Or shall the thing formed say of him who formed it, "He has no understanding"? NKJV

Chapter 11

Vessels of Wrath and of Mercy

Romans 9:22-24 introduces vessels of wrath and vessels of mercy. It is a continuing discussion about God's sovereignty and mercy. It is all about God and what He chooses to do. *Exodus 33:19 (NKJV)* states, *"Then He said, "I will make all My goodness pass before you, and I will proclaim the name of the LORD before you. I will be gracious to whom I will be gracious, and I will have compassion on whom I will have compassion."* Because the sovereign God of the universe stated, *"I am that I am;"* we therefore, as the created beings, must accept what He says in faith without questioning His sovereignty *(Rom 9:19-20)*.

The *18th chapter of Jeremiah* gives us a wonderful example of the potter and the clay, along with an explanation of God's sovereign nature. Even within God's sole discretion to do what He chooses, He has not terminated man's obligation within His mercy. Paul, knowing the OT Scriptures well, brought forth this example once again, because most Jews knew it well and could readily relate. Just as God controls the heart of the king *(Prov*

21:1), so goes the will of His divine hand. He is God, and He is in the very details of His plan and purpose. He does not miss a jot or tittle. Even though man still has an obligation to respond, God has not relinquished His control, not in the least. For the Lord has made everything for Himself, even the wicked for the day of doom (*Prov 16:4*).

Paul ends the *9th chapter of Romans* with a discussion regarding the mystery of how God adopted the Gentiles, and how they have now become His people. He also shares how the Cross is a stumbling block for Israel. Paul further recites passages from Isaiah and Hosea, as Scriptures to support his declarations. Thus, when Paul opens the *10th chapter of Romans*, he is still reflecting on the fact that even though Israel was as great as the *"sand of the sea"* only a remnant will be saved. He says, *"Brethren, my heart's desire and prayer to God for Israel is that they may be saved. 2 For I bear them witness that they have a zeal for God, but not according to knowledge. 3 For they being ignorant of God's righteousness, and seeking to establish their own righteousness, have not submitted to the righteousness of God" (Rom 10:1-3).*

Remember, the *first three chapters of Romans* tells us the outcome of what happens to men when they seek after and establish their own righteousness; God turns them over to themselves and they are condemned because they'd rather believe a lie than the truth. Paul, now specifically states, that even though the Jews have a desire to want to serve God, they are doing it without knowledge of Him and therefore their worship is unacceptable. Since they refuse to believe the truth and believe their own self-righteousness, their response to what God has done is still death; even though they are the chosen nation. God, during the dispensation of Grace deals with each individual, not a nation (*Rom 10:12-13*). After the Church is raptured, Israel will become the main focal point again and God will judge the nations. It is Paul's desire during this dispensation that all Jews come into the knowledge of their Messiah, Jesus the Christ. God is still saving some Jews during this dispensation, "The Age of Grace/Church" (*Rom 11:1-5*).

God is faithful (*Deut 7:9*). He will perform His side of a covenant (a contract which cannot be broken), despite the other side breaching theirs. God will do what He said He will do because His promise is unconditional. God, during the fourth dispensation made a promise to Abraham in Genesis 12 that his seed would be as plentiful as the sand and stars. The sand in this Scripture represents Abraham's earthly seed, the Israelites. It was God's plan for Israel to tell the whole world about Him, so that others would know of His goodness and His greatness. The stars represent God's spiritual seed, and include both Jews and Gentiles who represent *"The Body of Christ"*.

Even though God has not broken His covenant with Israel, He has punished them for their disobedience. During their punishment, God has placed the Jews on hold as a nation and God has allowed a time for the Gentiles to be grafted into His Body (*Rom 11:11*). This is referred to as *"the fullness of the Gentiles" found in Romans 11:26*. To reiterate, during the Dispensation of Grace, which we are living in now; God is dealing with Jews and Gentiles collectively (*Rom 10: 12-13*). Yes, God is angry with Israel, but they have not stopped being His chosen nation. After the Age of Grace, God will take His finger off of the pause button and resume His dealings with Israel as a nation, during the Tribulation Period. Israel will have the opportunity once again to embrace their role and share the good news of God with the world during this time (*Rev 7:2-8*). Both Gentiles and Jews are commissioned to evangelize the world.

In every dispensation, God has a remnant of believers who will serve Him and keep His commandments. Paul reminds us by using a passage from *I Kings 19:10-14* that God always has a remnant set aside. Even Paul, a murderer selected to be an Apostle to the Gentiles, is proving that God is not through with Israel. Even at the end of the Tribulation Period, all of Israel will be saved; specifically those who have made it through the end of the period and did not take the mark of the beast.

Rom 12:1-2

I beseech you therefore, brethren, by the mercies of God, that you present your bodies a living sacrifice, holy, acceptable to God, which is your reasonable service. 2 And do not be conformed to this world, but be transformed by the renewing of your mind, that you may prove what is that good and acceptable and perfect will of God. (NKJV)

We have reviewed the first eight doctrinal chapters; and the three dispensational chapters. The last devotional *chapters of Romans 12-16* deal with our duty. After we have been taught the truth, we then need to practice living it. Dr. Jimmy Hayes said it well in his lecture, "Precepts Must Have Practice!" Paul begins the duty portion of Scripture with an urging to the Body of Christ: since God has shown His ultimate love toward us, we need to give our lives back to Him which is the most sensible thing to do. Upon hearing the phrase "living sacrifice," it almost seems like an oxymoron because sacrifices are presented for death (*Lev 1:3*). But this is exactly what God wants us to do. He wants us to die to self, so that He may live through us (*II Cor 4:11*). As Christians we must learn to die daily, so that Christ may rule and reign in our members.

We are told to renew our minds and be not conformed to this world. Putting on the mind of Christ requires us to read His Scriptures daily to learn how to submit ourselves to Him. We learn how to die effectively, so that He may live through us efficiently (*Phil 1:21*). This is a present continuous act.

Many Theologians differ on whether there are actually 3 degrees of God's will. If the position is taken from a viewpoint of sanctification, one can easily see how Christians move from one good degree of grace to another. Positionally speaking, using the degrees of salvation, it is *good* that we are saved from the penalty of sin, and are in the process being saved from the power (sanctification-*acceptable*) because it is a process. In the *perfect* place of His will, we will be saved from the very presence of sin (glorification-*perfect*) because our glorified bodies are now able to rule and reign with Him. In this example, we see the life of the believer and how he progresses within God's decree that His children will conform to the image of His Son (*Rom 8:29*).

The *first two verses of Romans 12* tells believers how our attitudes are to be toward God. Once we understand this concept, God starts working on our heart so that we may see how our attitudes should be toward our fellow man as reflected in *verses 3-13*. Right smack in the middle of understanding how to treat our fellow man, we find *Romans 12:9*. This verse emphasizes the word "love." Christians should show love in all that they do as they conform to the likeness of God's Son (*Rom 8:29*). God is love (*I Jn 4:8,16*) and we want to emulate not only our Creator, but our Father. Love, an action verb, stresses that believers should be transparent in this action and pure in their motive.

Paul cites a few of the *Ten Commandments*. In *Romans 13:9-10* he shows when love is enacted, it fulfills the law. When we do what the *Ten Commandments* state, it is summed up in the word "love." Paul goes on to share that love should not only be transparent, but it should also be disgusted by evil and cling to good. When love is present, it's like a well that is overflowing with tenderness, kindness, and affection toward one another. The attributes of love are continued through the remainder of the chapter and echoed beautifully in *I Corinthians 13*; love never fails.

Paul also uses contrasting thoughts to emphasize how important love is. So if one loves evil, then God is not in Him for God is love (*Jn 4:16*). Likewise, if we choose not to practice all the things that love requires, it presupposes that God is not in us either.

Isa 43:1

But now, thus says the LORD, who created you, O Jacob, And He who formed you, O Israel:"Fear not, for I have redeemed you;I have called you by your name; You are Mine. NKJV

Chapter 12

Recurring Themes

Recurring themes run throughout the Word of God. Only two will be highlighted in this chapter, "election" and "the order of things." In studying *Romans*, God inspires Paul to explain the importance of His elections; His called ones. He initially called Abram from his country and family to a land that God would show him. From Abraham's seed, only one was elected as *"the son of the promise,"* Isaac. Isaac's younger son, Jacob, produces the line of "the Promised One." In light of what we just learned, it can be safely stated that *Romans 9:12-13* is a summary statement for verses 6-11 —God chose these men before birth; therefore, it could not be about works. God began establishing election during the Old Testament. This theme appears throughout the Bible.

Another recurring theme that seems adjacent to election which belongs to God's natural law is "the order of things." In His natural law, things are first natural, then spiritual. Man is born into the natural world, yet has to be reborn to the spiritual. The natural seed is shown first, Cain, then Abel, represents the spiritual seed because his offering was accepted. The first Adam is the natural man, and Jesus, the last Adam is the spiritual man. The natural man represents the flesh. The spiritual man has a regenerated spirit. God hates the work of the flesh (*Gal 5:19*), but loves the work of the Holy Spirit (*Gal 5:22*). When reading Romans the ninth chapter, we must understand the significance of this law. God is not only invoking the law of order, but also election, even within Abraham's family. Everyone that is of Abraham's seed has not been elected to receive the promise. Only those coming from Isaac's line (*Gen 17:19*) are recipients of the promise. Every human who has been created is not automatically a child of God. Only the created humans who have been elected are His children. This passage of Scripture is once again affirming election and the natural order of things. God chose the younger over the elder even before they were brought forth in time or born (*Gen 25:23*). The greater prophecy is that God wants His children to allow the Spirit to lead and let the flesh be a servant to the Holy Spirit (*Rom 8:10, 14; Gal 3:1*).

There are three distinct people groups in the Bible indicated in the first chapter of John: the *Nations (Jn 10b)*, the *children of Israel (Jn 11)*, the *Body of Christ (Jn 12-13)*. The Scripture says:

John 1:10-13
He was in the world, and the world was made through Him, and the world did not know Him. ¹¹ He came to His own, and His own did not receive Him. ¹² But as many as received Him, to them He gave the right to become children of God, to those who believe in His name: ¹³ who were born, not of blood, nor of the will of the flesh, nor of the will of man, but of God.

This passage of Scripture beautifully illustrates election. God says that He will bless those who bless the seed of the promise, and curse those who curse them (*Gen 12:3*). Ishmael's and Esau's descendants as nations were not of the "promise" and therefore, did not walk with God (*Gen 17:18-21, Mal 1:1-5*). God is sovereign and does what He wants, when He wants, and to whom He chooses. His election and His law of order stand throughout all dispensations.

1 Sam 15:22

And Samuel said, Hath the LORD as great delight in burnt offerings and sacrifices, as in obeying the voice of the LORD? Behold, to obey is better than sacrifice, and to hearken than the fat of rams. KJV

Chapter 13

Basic Principles Prevail

One of the basic principles of the Bible is obedience.
Throughout the hallowed pages, God has breathed its
importance, even to the smallest degree. Everyone has heard
this paraphrased quote in one form or the other, *"render unto
Caesar what is Caesar's..."* (*Matt 22:21*). God wanted us to
know without a shadow of doubt that He is in control of all
things, including governments. In the thirteenth chapter of
Romans, Paul lays out our civil duties as believers. Because we
are under God's subjection, this makes us subject to all
governments and systems which He has put in place. We are to
respect governments and others who have charge over us. This
is within God's divine decree for our lives as believers. In
obeying government control, we are also obliged to pay any
taxes that have been placed upon us. When we fail to do so, we
are disobeying God and committing sin. God is clear; if we want
to have peace and harmony with authorities, then obey them. If
we want to be contrary to His will regarding obeying authorities,
peace will be removed and fear will replace it *(Rom 13:2-4)*.

Our debt to our fellow man (neighbor) is to love them as we love ourselves which fulfills the law toward man *(Rom 13:8-10)*. We are also supposed to obey God by loving Him with all our heart, soul, mind, and strength *(Mk 12:30)*. God has given to us this example in *Romans 5:8, "But God commendeth His love toward us, in that, while we were yet sinners, Christ died for us." (KJV)* Christ, because of love, died for us and we can never repay this debt. So with Christ being our ultimate example, we are to do likewise.

"Suffer the little children to come unto me, and forbid them not:. . . " (Mk 10:14) is what Jesus said to His disciples. This beautiful Scripture was not just an object lesson about the kingdom of God at that exact moment, but a poignant fact about the importance of protecting little children, both in the physical and in the spiritual. Paul expands on this in his object lesson in the *14th chapter of Romans.* Mature Christians are instructed not to tear down immature Christians on issues that don't matter as much as getting the points of salvation right. Paul uses those that are "weak in the faith" as a synonym for "little children in the faith." Stronger Christians, must bear the infirmities of the weak *(Rom 15:1)* and protect them by learning not to argue or make a point about the small things pertaining to food or days.

This object lesson is not just limited to food or days of the week, but any issue in which Christians differ. During Paul's ministry the issue was food and days of the week. Even though these same issues persist today; others have been added to our coffers, such as: predestination or free will, post or pre-tribulation, serving the Lord's Supper anytime or just on the 1st Sunday of every month, to drink or not to drink, to gamble or not to gamble, and to dance or not to dance. These are just a few, but there are many, many more. It is more important to encourage a brother who is weaker, than being right on these small matters. The more mature Christian must not forget what he knows and believes, but rather be compassionate in his or her approach. He displays Christ-likeness toward young eyes and ears that don't fully understand that they are free in Christ Jesus. All things may be lawful but may not be expedient (*I Cor 6:12*).

Paul's message then and now is, "don't sweat the small stuff." If there be any contention between believers, it should be for withstanding the faith, as Paul had to do when he withstood Peter regarding salvation (*Gal 2:11-21*). On this point alone, mature loving believers should help their weaker brothers to gain the full understanding of Paul's teaching.

We then who are strong ought to bear with the scruples of the weak, and not to please ourselves. 2 Let each of us please his neighbor for his good, leading to edification. 3 For even Christ did not please Himself; but as it is written, "The reproaches of those who reproached You fell on Me." (Rom 15:1-3 NKJV).

The first few *verses of chapter 15* continue the examination of the Law of Love. The Christian life is one of sacrifice, as seen by the ultimate sacrifice Himself, Jesus. In the Garden of Gethsemane, Jesus gave us the highest example of love when He submitted Himself to the Father's will, *"O My Father, if it is possible, let this cup pass from Me; nevertheless, not as I will, but as You will." (Matt 26:39).* Jesus knew the agonizing pain that He was about to experience. Yes, the death of the cross was going to be humiliating and excruciating. But that was not even the bitter cup to which He was referring. Even though the physical part of this experience was going to be horrible, it did not compare to the anguish He was experiencing–knowing that He had to be separated from the Father for a time. For love's sake, Jesus had decided to relinquish His will and do the will of His Father. Jesus bore our infirmities because we were too weak and needed a Savior.

Jesus has presented the two-fold pattern in which we should follow: submit our will to the Father and bear the infirmities of the weak (*Matt 8:17, 22:37-39*). Christians should keep this in mind when viewing other believers' needs, and place their own needs at a lower priority. When this Christian practice is exercised, Christ is lifted up and the babe in Christ sees how Christ would like to one day work in his or her life. This exhorts and builds up the young believer.

Therefore, if we love God with our whole heart, and love our neighbors as ourselves; we as believers will receive each other in the like manner which Christ exemplified for us on Calvary. For now there is no difference between the Jew and the Greek; the veil has been rent from top to bottom, and we are no longer outsiders because Christ has become our Mediator. Praise be to God for His tender mercies!

In *verses 16 and 17 of Romans 16*, Paul urges us to note the people who are causing divisions and are trying to trap others with false doctrine. Believers are to be aware of them and are to shun them. This is in distinct contrast as to how we are to receive believers as instructed in the previous chapter. God is a God of black and white; there is no gray area for Him. You are either in His camp or you are in satan's. You are either walking in the marvelous light or you are walking in darkness.

Satan is the master deceiver and is very cunning and subtle in his approach. He is so crafty, that he has tricked the world into believing that he and his demons will show up with a frightening and diabolical appearance as depicted in movies. This is far from the truth. Shrewd satan's appearance is quite deceptive so much so that he and his workforce transform their appearance into that of an "angel of light" (*II Cor 11:14-15*).

With this cunningness in mind, Paul warns us how satan will target the Body of Christ from within and without. Satan uses people who go to church but aren't in the Body of Christ as his emissaries. They are positioned within the church to appear as Christians. But because they don't really serve the true God, their demonic nature will eventually be exposed. These workers of iniquity may know the Word, and often can quote Scripture better than some true believers; yet they misquote Scripture and weave lies into it. Look at the woven craftiness in the Garden of Eden, when satan took God's Word regarding the fruit of the Tree of Knowledge of Good and Evil and put his own spin on it: God said, *"Of every tree of the garden you may freely eat; 17 but of the tree of the knowledge of good and evil you shall not eat, for in the day that you eat of it you shall surely die."* (Gen 2:16-17). Satan spin to Eve was: *"Has God indeed said, 'You shall not eat of every tree of the garden?"* (Gen 3:1). To a babe in Christ, or untrained Christian, the deception is not readily detectable. It almost sounds like satan said the same thing as God. Taking a closer look at the Scripture, we do indeed see that it is not the same.

In addition, satan does his greatest deceptive work when it pertains to the doctrine of salvation. He loves to mix up the simplicity of the message with <u>faith plus something</u>. The devil uses man's pride and sinful nature as an avenue in which to deceive *"through the lust of the flesh, the lust of the eyes, and the pride of life..."* (I Jn 2:16).

The devil's subtle tactics are used over and over again, not just within the church walls, but also outside of the church walls. One of the heresies that has been floating around modern Christendom is today's "ecumenical" perversity and "politically correctness" which promote "that all roads lead to Christ." This is definitely a doctrine from the pit of hell. Jesus was adamant when He said, *"I am the Way, the Truth, and the Life: no man cometh unto the Father, but by Me." (Jn 14:6).* This statement is emphatic! Jesus Christ is the <u>only way</u> and does not validate "all or many roads" lead to the Father. He is the only road; just by Him and Him alone. Amen.

Eph 4:11-12, 14

And He Himself gave some to be apostles, some prophets, some evangelists, and some pastors and teachers, 12 for the equipping of the saints for the work of ministry ... 14 that we should no longer be children, tossed to and fro and carried about with every wind of doctrine , by the trickery of men, in the cunning craftiness of deceitful plotting ...

NKJV

Part 2

Divisive Doctrines

Scripture is so rich and the depths are unfathomable because *The Word* is a living document. The doctrinal truths in *Romans* are the springboard that furthers our growth and understanding. *God's Word is Christ (Jn 1:1-2);* the ultimate platform of enumerable foundational doctrines. Included within these immeasurable teachings are several subjects in which Christendom depart in belief and understanding. Some of these subjects cause division such as: the doctrines of Baptism, the Canon, The Trinity, Election, The Lord's Supper, Salvation, Eternal Security, Predestination, and the Last Things, etc.

These major themes in Christianity have divided the Church since its inception. One would think that we would be more unified, especially since Christ prayed for unity and the Holy Spirit lives in the believer. Remembering what was discussed earlier in chapters about man's two natures; there will always be a struggle because of his sin nature. Regardless of the denomination, each one thinks their doctrine is sound and morally correct. Conversely, when we get to heaven, denominational fallacies and faulty reasoning will be revealed. The Lord admonishes us through Paul's example when he had to confront Peter. We may not agree on every doctrinal position; however, when it is pertaining to *The Gospel* (His death, burial, and resurrection, according to Scripture *(I Cor 15:3-4))*; we are to defend *The Gospel* at all cost *(Gal 2:11-16)*. The mantra must be, "Faith plus nothing!" Jesus paid it all. Yet, man's hubris (his pride) constantly seeps through and puffs up his own works. Although justification is a substantial topic, we won't be covering it at this time.

Only a few divisive doctrines have been chosen to examine for this book. These divisive doctrinal selections are: <u>Salvation Security (Eternal Security)</u>, <u>Election</u>, and <u>Free Will</u>.

Elements of each selection's point of view will be from our highest authority, the Scriptures; yet still reflecting a Baptist gaze. The Scripture's authority, having the highest hierarchy, renders Scriptures to interpret Scripture. This is of utmost importance; thereby allowing Christians to reason with one another. While reviewing these topics, we will explore:

1. How does each doctrine relate to each other?
2. Do any of the doctrines oppose the other doctrines or do they all work in concert?

3. Can the accuracy of the selected doctrines be proven with Scripture?

Continued utilization of The New Hampshire Declaration of Faith will be used as a resource for addressing these diverging views. The discussion of salvation proper and its various properties are seen throughout several of the articles. *(See Appendix C, page169)*

Rom 8:37-39

For I am persuaded that neither death nor life, nor angels nor principalities nor powers, nor things present nor things to come, 39 nor height nor depth, nor any other created thing, shall be able to separate us from the love of God which is in Christ Jesus our Lord.

NKJV

Chapter 14

Salvation Security

A principal source of contention within the Baptist faith and throughout Christendom is the question regarding Salvation Security or Eternal Salvation. Is our salvation secure or can it be lost? Two opposing sides will be examined in chapter 16 in further scrutinizing this question. Let's consider a plausible framework with which to discuss Salvation Security. <u>The Tenses of Salvation</u> <u>Chart</u> (shown on the next page) is a helpful place to begin when studying the Scriptures. *"Rightly dividing the Word of Truth," (II Tim 2:14-15)* is necessary in order to accurately answer the security question. The chart shows Salvation in tenses: *past, present, and future* which depicts its operation in a believer's life.

TENSES OF SALVATION CHART

Past	Present	Future
SALVATION *One time act*	SANCTIFICATION *Daily process*	GLORIFICATION *Future act*
Saved from the	*Being saved from the*	*One day will be saved from the very*
PENALTY	POWER	PRESENCE
JUSTIFICATION	SANCTIFICATION	GLORIFICATION
CONVERSION	CONVERSATION	COMMUNION
POSITION	PROGRESSION	PERMANENCE (ULTIMATE)
MY SPIRIT	MY SOUL	MY BODY
RELATIONSHIP	FELLOWSHIP	CO-REIGNSHIP

SALVATION is a one-time act that doesn't reoccur. The old adage, "once saved always saved," hails from this occurrence. Christ's finished work at the cross saved us once and for all *(Heb 7:26-27, 9:11-12 & 25-28, 10:10,12,14; Rom 8:38-39)*. After His salvific work was completed, He sat at the right hand of God the Father *(Eph 1:15-23)*. When we accept the calling, we are immediately saved from the penalty of sin, which is death *(Rom 6:23)*. We are justified and made righteous in the sight of God. We have been converted from death to life. We have positionally moved from outside the Body of Christ to now being in Christ by the power of the Holy Spirit. Our spirits have been quickened (made alive) and we have been adopted as sons of God *(Rom 8:14-17, Gal 3:26-29)*.

<u>SANTIFICATION</u> is a daily process in which we are being saved from the very power of sin. Earlier in *chapter 9* we discussed the mechanism and how this is possible. *Galatians 5:16* reminds us to allow the Holy Spirit to lead us, thereby walking in the Spirit, so we won't succumb to the power of the flesh. Sanctify means to "set apart," the same word in the Greek is "holy" (ἅγιος, *hagios*). Just as items were set aside for the Levitical priests for the Tabernacle and Temple worship; we should do likewise and be set aside for daily service. Our bodies are the temple of the Holy Spirit *(I Cor 3:16; II Cor 6:16)* and we should present them accordingly *(Rom 12:1-2)*. Our conversation changes when we constantly renew our minds. During our pilgrimage here on earth, we are constantly dealing with two natures which are warring against each other *(Gal 5:17)*. In *II Corinthians the tenth chapter*, we get a better understanding about this war. This war is a spiritual one that can only be won by the Holy Spirit. Growing in the fear and admonition of the Lord equips us to lay down our lives and consciously choose not to grieve the Holy Spirit *(Eph 4:30)*.

First Corinthians 2:14 further testifies that a believer can commit acts of the flesh *(Gal 5:16)* when the believer is not being led by the Spirit. The Holy Spirit is the only one who can overcome the lusts of the flesh *(Gal 5:19-21)*. This transpires because a natural man cannot receive the truths of the Spirit for they are foolish to him. A natural man doesn't have the Spirit of God, but a carnal Christian does. A carnal Christian is one who has believed the Gospel, but remains a babe in Christ *(I Cor 3:1)*. A babe in Christ has not grown from his initial state of salvation. He has chosen not to submit to the Holy Spirit by putting on the full Armor of God which is Christ Jesus. He therefore, will succumb to acts of the flesh by not willingly submitting to the sanctification process of the Holy Spirit. Our souls (mind, will and emotions) will sincerely yearn to be with the Lord, as we conform, as God promised, into the image of our Savior, Christ Jesus *(Rom 8:29)*.

GLORIFICATION is when we will be saved from the very presence of sin. When we receive our glorified bodies we will no longer be conflicted with the two natures. We will be changed in the twinkling of an eye; put on incorruption and immortality; to commune with Christ forever (permanence), and co-reign with Him *(Rom 8:23, Phil 3:20-21, I Cor 15:42-44, 15:52-53, II Cor 5:1-5, Jn 3:2, II Tim 2:11-13)*.

Confirmation is comforting in knowing that Jesus completely saved us. Salvation and sanctification often get confused. When this confusion arises, one believes he can lose his salvation. The Tenses of Salvation explain, illustrate, and strengthens the fact that salvation indeed cannot be lost. Many people are familiar with *John 3:16* yet fail to read through to *verse 3:18*. This verse states that if one does not believe in Him, he is already condemned. Scripture continues to support believing on the Son gains one eternal life *(I Jn 5:11-13)*. Deeds nor works, nor rituals gain this blessing. The *"coup de grâce"* further confirms that we don't have anything to do with getting or losing our salvation. Read Jesus' prayer in *John 17.* Jesus shares that all whom the Father has given Him have believed and He has lost none of them! Glory hallelujah, what a wonderful reason to shout!

Salvation Security is one of the controversial doctrines Christians have struggled with for centuries. Let's continue to move forward and explore the other two divisive teachings selected which are closely related to Salvation Security. Salvation Security or the loss thereof appears to align with the other selected doctrines. Many similar Scripture references may be utilized, discerned, and dissected differently by the power of the Holy Spirt. God reminds us that His Word is sharper than any two-edge sword with the ability to divide the soul and spirit *(Heb 4:12).* Contextual concepts further confirm that Scripture does not lie, nor is it confusing. Scripture always supports what it has previously been stated.

Chapter 15

Election and Free Will

The conflicting views of Election and Free Will are as polarizing as Salvation Security; and yet they are quite often used in tandem. The New Hampshire Declaration of Faith *Article Nine* presents the doctrines of *Election and Free Will* as existing harmoniously within the framework of God's sovereignty. This article states:

> *We believe that <u>Election</u> is the eternal purpose of God, according to which he graciously regenerates, sanctifies, and saves sinners; <u>that being perfectly consistent with the free agency of man</u>, it comprehends all the means in connection with the end; that it is a most glorious display of God's sovereign goodness, being infinitely free, wise, holy, and unchangeable; that it utterly excludes boasting, and promotes humility, love, prayer, praise, trust in God, and active imitation of his free mercy; that it encourages the use of means in the highest degree; that it may be ascertained by its effects in all who truly believe the gospel; that it is the foundation of Christian*

assurance; and that to ascertain it with regard to ourselves demands and deserves the utmost diligence. [2]

The New Hampshire Declaration of Faith has a comprehensive view of Scripture, thereby eloquently expressed in the ninth article. Yet the question still arises in so many Theological circles as to which one is true? Is *Election* the sole ideal to the detriment of *Free Will*? Or is *Free Will* the champion to the loser of the *Election* camp? Or can the position be taken in which they both are true completely but to varying degrees? In order for the discourse to move forward, let us consider frequently used words surrounding these polarizing doctrines. Just having a common footing on what we are discussing will help us come to a better understanding as we reason with one another while contemplating Scriptural context.

Merriam-Webster's Collegiate Dictionary uses these definitions for the following words along with the Strong's Concordance numbers and corresponding Greek Words from The MacArthur Life Works Library/Libronix Digital Library System:

WORD/DEFINITION TABLE

WORD	DEFINITION	GREEK WORD
choice/choose	Select freely; decide; elect	ἐκλέγομαι (ĕklĕgŏmai, ek-leg´-om-ahee)
Strong's # and word usage	1586 "choose" 19 times, "choose out" once, and "make choice" once. **1** to pick out, or choose out for one's self.	

WORD	DEFINITION	GREEK WORD
Decree	**An order, having the force of law; judicial decision; to command; to determine or order**	δόγμα (dŏgma, dog′-mah)
Strong's # and word usage	1378 Five occurrences; translates as "decree" three times, and "ordinance" twice. **1** doctrine, decree, ordinance. 1A of public decrees	
Elect	**Select; to choose; chosen for salvation through divine mercy; set apart**	ἐκλεκτός (ĕklĕktŏs, ek-lek-tos)
Strong's # and word usage	1588 23 occurrences; translates as "elect" 16 times, and "chosen" seven times. **1** picked out, chosen. 1A chosen by God,. *1A1* to obtain salvation through Christ. 1A1A Christians are called "chosen or elect" of God.	
foreknowledge	**Know beforehand; foresee; fact of being aware of information in front of, favor**	Πρόγνωσις (prŏgnōsis, prog′-no-sis)
Strong's # and word usage	4268 Two occurrences; translates as "foreknowledge" twice. **1** foreknowledge. **2** forethought, pre-arrangement.	
Free	**Enjoying political and civil liberty or independence; capable of choosing for oneself; not hampered or restricted; capable of moving or turning in any direction; outspoken, separate**	ἐλεύθερος (ĕlĕuthĕrŏs, el-yoo′-ther-os)
Strong's # and word usage	1658 23 occurrences; translates as "free" 18 times, "free woman" three times, "at liberty" once, and "free man" once. **1** freeborn. 1A in a civil sense, one who is not a slave. 1B of one who ceases to be a slave, freed, manumitted. **2** free, exempt, unrestrained, not bound by an obligation. **3** in an ethical sense: free from the yoke of the Mosaic Law.	
predestinate	**To foreordain to an earthly or eternal lot or destiny by divine decree; appoint or settle beforehand**	Προορίζω (prŏŏrizō, prŏ-or-id′-zo)
Strong's # and word usage	4309 Six occurrences; translates as "predestinate" four times, "determine before" once, and "ordain" once. **1** to predetermine, decide beforehand. **2** in the NT of God	

WORD	DEFINITION	GREEK WORD
	decreeing from eternity. **3** to foreordain, appoint beforehand. (note: from 3724 and 4253 translates as "determine" twice, "ordain" twice, "as it was determined + 2596 + 3588" once, "declare" once, "limit" once, and "determine" once. **1** to define. **1A** to mark out the boundaries or limits (of any place or thing) 1b to determine, appoint. **1B1** that which has been determined, acc. to appointment, decree. **1B2** to ordain, determine, appoint. translates as "before" 44 times, "above" twice, "above … ago" once, and "or ever" once. **1** before.	
will (word 1)	**Desire; wish, disposition, inclination; determination; collective desire of group; consent**	Θέλημα (thelēma)
Strong's # and word usage	2307 64 occurrences; translates as "will" 62 times, "desire" once, and "pleasure" once. **1** what one wishes or has determined shall be done. **1A** of the purpose of God to bless mankind through Christ. **1B** of what God wishes to be done by us. **1B1** commands, precepts. **2** will, choice, inclination, desire, pleasure.	
will (word 2)	will, counsel, purpose to will, wish	Βούλομαι bŏulēma, boo´-lay-mah)
Strong's # and word usage	1013, 1014 34 occurrences; translates as "will" 15 times, "would" 11 times, "be minded" twice, "intend" twice, "be disposed" once, "be willing" once, "list" once, and "of his own will" once. **1** to will deliberately, have a purpose, be minded. **2** of willing as an affection, to desire.	

While studying these definitions, one can see that many of them have similar meanings and some are very closely related. *Will, desire, and decree* could possibly be used interchangeably; so could *call, choose or elect*; especially if utilizing the English language. However, in the Greek, *call, calling, and called* have become more personal; especially if the definite article is used.

"The called" is an invitation to the saints *(Rom 8:28)*. In Greek, d*esire* and *decree* have slightly different nuances that aren't readily articulated in English. Erwin Lutzer, in <u>The Doctrines that Divide</u>, explains the differences this way:

> But there is a difference between the decree of God and the desire of God. A moment's reflection will confirm this distinction. Think of it this way: God did not delight in the death of His Son. We could say that He was not willing that His Son die and suffer in agony upon the cross. Yet, He decreed that it would happen. Christ died at the hands of wicked men doing whatsoever God's hand "predestined to occur" *(Acts 4:28)*. Clearly, God chose to forego His desires. He desired one thing but decreed another. If we ask why, all that we can do is reply that He had an overriding purpose to accomplish; and that purpose overshadowed His desire to see Christ exempt from suffering.
>
> Similarly, He desires that all men be saved. Yet, on the other hand, He allows the greater part of humanity to perish. We simply do not know why He has chosen to forgo His desire to see all men be saved. We can be quite sure, however, that there is some ultimate purpose, for the Scripture says, "The Lord has made everything for its own purpose, even the wicked for the day of evil" *(Prov 16:4)*. [3]

The clarity that has been given from Lutzer will be the basis when using these words. Also, *choose* or *elect* are similar words that use the same prefix *"ek"* which means "called out," or "from." Predestinate and foreknowledge use the Greek prefix, "pro" meaning "before." In looking at the word *"predestinate"* we see that it originally comes from two Greek words that mean "declare beforehand." *Romans 8:29-30* uses the word "predestinate." In the deliberate mind of God, He foreknew or favored in "eternity past" how He wanted His decree for mankind to line up in "time" and in "eternity future" God is outside of time and chose how to deal with man during specific time periods throughout Holy Writ. Within the Holy Scriptures, God has given us a snapshot of His divine decree. <u>God's perfect will</u>–which is His divine decree, resides within His sovereignty and must be fulfilled. <u>God's permissive will</u>–which is His desire, also resides within His sovereignty, however God allows for a multitude of paths to occur in which to fulfill His purpose. Man's will is also designated in His permissive will. Later in Part 3 we will continue to dig further to learn more about man's will in relation to God's will, by applying the insights presented in *Romans*.

With this understanding, we can envision the possibility for Election and Free Will to both be true; and how confusion could arise without this perspective. We have not been made privy to the entire working knowledge of how God intermingles His perfect and permissive wills; yet we know that His ways are higher than our ways *(Isa 55:8-9)*, so we learn to trust *(Rom 15:13)* by faith *(Heb 11:1-11)* (πίστις [*pistis* /**pis**·tis/]. This essential word "faith" in the Greek has over 200 occurrences (which is mentioned 39 times in *Romans*) and speaks of: *belief and fidelity; conviction or belief respecting man's relationship to God and divine things; the conviction that God exists and is the creator and ruler of all things, the provider and bestower of eternal salvation through Christ.* 4

Spiritual insight is being revealed. *Predestinate* is not really a true synonym for *election*, although it is akin to it. *Predestinate* is tied more directly with the sanctification process— "conforming to Jesus," than the salvation reception. The *call, election or choice* is more related to salvation. At the time we are saved, "born again," several things occur simultaneously—we are rejuvenated, indwelt, baptized, and sealed, yet these are separate actions. We will continue to scrutinize these concepts in the following chapters. God chose us and determined that we would be conforming to Jesus' image. "Conforming" as used previously denotes the present tense of sanctification; it is active motion happening now. Yet in the mind of God, it is shown in Scripture as past tense "conformed" because it has already been decreed. We know the Bible is the inerrant *Word of God*; this is the absolute conclusion. God's election and predestination is His perfect will—His sovereign decree.

Man's free will, which is housed in God's permissive will, falls within the purpose and plan of God. Examining man's will and how it is shaped through diverging poles, will help us formulate where we position ourselves between the poles and how we steadfastly uphold our beliefs.

Chapter 16

Diverging Poles

Polarizing concepts have been forming since the Church began. Remember some followed Paul and some Peter, not understanding that both were following Christ! Man's "stubborn will" causes schisms to develop throughout Christendom. Some schisms are extremely dangerous. Satan, the author of confusion, is the chief culprit who works through the pride of man to destroy the Church. Let's do a small review on how the Calvinism and Arminianism poles were created. This is not a complete Church history and denomination formation. It is however, the foundation on which we gain a better understanding of how poles were formed and where our belief systems reside in relation to salvation security, election, and free will.

Harold L. Fickett, Jr. in his <u>A Layman's Guide to Baptist Beliefs</u>" shares that "Baptists are considered Calvinists even though we predate John Calvin in history and do not base our doctrines on his writings, but rather on the *Word of God*." [5] Let's carefully examine pathways that have divided denominations for centuries.

As stated in Lewis Sperry Chafer's book, Major Bible Themes,

> Systems of human thought have tended to go either to one extreme where God's sovereign purpose is made absolute or to another extreme of magnifying the freedom of man until God is no longer in control. [6]

This systemic debate has been going on since our early Church fathers started pondering the Scriptures. In his book, The Doctrines that Divide, Erwin Lutzer presents the debates through the centuries, starting with Augustine and Pelagius. Augustine was a Theologian from Hippo in Northern Africa. Pelagius was a British monk. Augustine's position was that he was totally helpless, and that if God wanted His will realized, then God Himself would have to make it so. Pelagius took strong opposition to Augustine's stance. Pelagius believed that when man was faced with a choice of whether to sin or not, man could choose to do right or wrong.

Throughout history these distinctive views polarized Christianity. Augustine, Luther, Calvin and Whitefield adhered to the total depravity of man, with the work of salvation existing in God's hand alone. On the other side, Pelagius, Erasmus, Arminius, and Wesley discounted God's sovereignty and insisted that God depends on man's choice for salvation, which was labeled a works proposition from their opposition. Jack W. Cottrell, in <u>Perspectives on Election</u> shares this view about classical predestination:

> As I am using this term, it is the view that before the world ever existed God conditionally predestined some specific individuals to eternal life and the rest to eternal condemnation, based on his foreknowledge of their freewill responses to his law and to his grace. [7]

Cottrell obviously takes an Arminian position in his statement. In light of our understanding of the Word Study presented on "election" and "predestination;" they should not be used interchangeably within the context of the Tenses of Salvation. To reiterate, salvation corresponds with election and sanctification corresponds with conforming to His Son.

<u>Arminian Theology, Myths and Realities</u>, authored by Roger E. Olson, presents the argument that more evangelicals are more Arminian in their positions than they realize because they champion Free Will. He also states that having an Arminian position has been misinterpreted by Theologians who really just don't understand the truth about Arminianism. Olson holds the premise that even though Arminianism heralded from Pelagius, it did not stay in its original form. *"Arminianism of the head"* and *"Arminianism of the heart"* are two opposing ideas as

presented by Alan Sell per Olsen. Sell's explains that
"...'*Arminianism of the head*' denies the total depravity and the
absolute necessity of supernatural grace for salvation." [8]
Whereas the "'*Arminianism of the heart*'--the subject of Olsen's
book, "is the original Arminianism of Arminius, Wesley and
their evangelical heirs; ...which do not deny the total depravity
but believes the absolute necessity of supernatural grace for
even the first exercise of a good will toward God. Olsen
contends the Arminians of the heart are true Arminians and not
the Remonstrants who strayed away from Jacob Arminius'
teachings and formed a more liberal position that glorified
reason and freedom (free will) over divine revelation and
supernatural grace. Olsen further states that Arminianism and
Calvinism are more alike than different and they only differ in a
few fundamental beliefs: eternal security, God's providence and
the degree of predestination. Olsen notes in his book, <u>The Latin
to English translation of the Remonstrance</u> (the summary of the
Arminian position) in a condensed version by English Scholar
A.W. Harrison:

> 1. That God, by an eternal and unchangeable
> decree in Christ before the world was, determined
> to elect from the fallen and sinning race to
> everlasting life those who through His grace
> believe in Jesus Christ and persevere in faith and
> obedience; and, on the contrary, had resolved to
> reject the converted and unbelievers to everlasting
> damnation *(John 3:36).*

2. That, in consequence of this, Christ the Savior of the world died for all and every man, so that He obtained, by the death on the cross, reconciliation and pardon for sin for all men; in such manner, however, that none but the faithful actually enjoyed the same *(John 3:16; I John 2:2)*.

3. That man could not obtain saving faith of himself for by the strength of his own free will, but stood in need of God's grace through Christ to be renewed in thought and will *(John 15:5)*.

4. That this grace was the cause of the beginning, progress and completion of man's salvation; insomuch that none could believe nor persevere in faith without this co-operating grace of God in Christ. As to the manner of the operation of that grace, however, it is not irresistible *(Acts 7:51)*.

5. That true believers had sufficient strength through the Divine grace to fight against Satan, sin, the world, their own flesh, and get the victory over them; but whether by negligence they might not apostatize from the true Faith, lose the happiness of a good conscience and forfeit that grace needed to be more fully inquired into according to *Holy Writ*. [9]

At first glance, these concepts appear benign and don't seem to possibly contradict Scripture because references have been provided. But a closer analysis of Biblical truth contradicts these concepts and raises a red flag. This red flag was raised during the early years of the church; and the debate continues, to cause denominational friction.

After the Remonstrance was published, proponents of Calvin's approach to salvation were developed over a six-month period, which encapsulates the full body of work that was wrenched. These five points at the Synod of Dordtrecht in 1618-19 addressed the concerns of the Arminian Remonstrance. Since the majority of Baptists are considered Calvinists, his TULIP acrostic will be used to contrast Baptist, Catholic, and Methodist faiths. It has been noted that Evangelicals closely follow the Arminian view; however, they will not be distinctly considered in any of the examples.

The table on the next page, by Dennis Bratcher depicts the differences between the two cohorts. The five points are a summary of the differences between the two poles, Calvinism and Arminianism. [10]

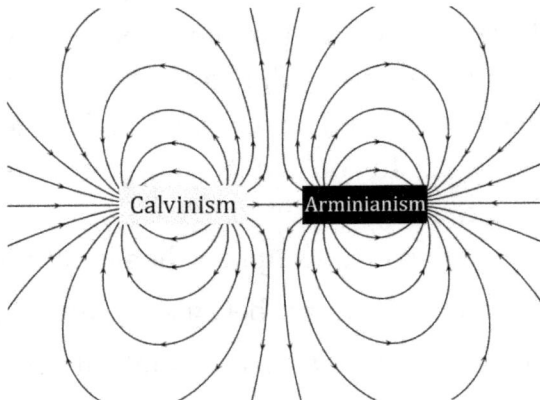

	John Calvin* Foundation laid by Augustine	John Wesley Foundation laid by Arminius
T	**Total Depravity -** Human beings are so affected by the negative consequences of original sin that they are incapable of being righteous, and are always and unchangeably sinful; human freedom is totally enslaved by sin so we can only choose evil.	**Deprivation -** Human beings are sinful and without God, incapable (deprived) on their own of being righteous; however, they are not irredeemably sinful and can be transformed by God's grace; God's prevenient grace restores to humanity the freedom of will.
U	**Unconditional Election -** Since human beings cannot choose for themselves, God by His eternal decree has chosen or elected some to be counted as righteous, without any conditions being placed on that election.	**Conditional Election -** God has chosen that all humanity be righteous by His grace, yet has called us to respond to that grace by exercising our God-restored human freedom as a condition of fulfilling election.
L	**Limited Atonement -** The effects of the Atonement, by which God forgave sinful humanity, are limited only to those whom He has chosen.	**Unlimited Atonement -** The effects of the Atonement are freely available to all those whom He has chosen, which includes all humanity, "whosoever will."
I	**Irresistible Grace -** The grace that God extends to human beings to the effect, their election cannot be refused, since it has been decreed by God.	**Resistible Grace -** God's grace is free and offered without merit; however, human beings have been granted freedom by God and can refuse His grace.
P	**Perseverance of the Saints -** Since God has decreed the elect, and they cannot resist grace, they are unconditionally and eternally secure in that election.	**Assurance and Security -** There is security in God's grace that allows assurance of salvation, but that security is in relation to continued faithfulness; we can still defiantly reject God.

Rev 22:18-19

For I testify to everyone who hears the words of the prophecy of this book: If anyone adds to these things, God will add to him the plagues that are written in this book; 19 and if anyone takes away from the words of the book of this prophecy, God shall take away his part from the Book of Life, from the holy city, and from the things which are written in this book. NKJV

Chapter 17

A Few TULIP Denominational Views

As stated before, these schools of thought constantly divide theologians and denominations. Roman Catholics and Methodists align themselves with Arminius' views; whereas Baptists more align with Calvin's views. Olsen reminds us that even though TULIP was given as an answer to the Remonstrance; Wesleyan Arminianism is more closely aligned with classical Arminianism. Let's juxtapose Catholics and Methodists against TULIP.

Total Depravity. Roman Catholics believe in the depravity of man but not in the total depravity of man. Catholics believe that a saving grace must intervene, based upon some inherent good in man. Methodists also believe in prevenient grace that allows man the ability to accept or reject the Gospel. Whereas Baptists believe that man is spiritually dead, Roman Catholics and Methodists believe that man is just spiritually sick and not dead. Does man's spirit need to be quickened and reborn or just healed? The thought that man is just sick and not spiritually dead totally contradicts Scripture. The book of *Romans* unequivocally shows us the answer to this question. Thus, the ultimate question is, "do we believe God, or do we believe man?" Nevertheless, one can see how the Roman Catholics are easily lead astray because they choose not to believe in *"sola Scriptura,"*--meaning the Bible alone. [11] Roman Catholics believe that the pope can speak on God's behalf and therefore speak actual Scripture into existence as if the pope is a part of the Godhead. God has made this clear that we are not to add to His Word *(Rev 22:18)*. With this faulty man-made logic, Scripture is misinterpreted and many Catholics have been led astray by not following Scripture alone. This faulty logic convinces them that there is some inherent good in man and that good men will choose God. Roman Catholics refute the sin nature *(Rom 5:12)* that was passed down by Adam as the federal headship of the human race.

John Wesley, the father of the Methodist denomination wholeheartedly adopted James Arminius' views and believed that God gave enough grace to spark man's Free Will to allow man to choose Him. Lutzer said of Wesley in the <u>Doctrines that Divide</u>:

> It seemed so plain to Wesley that Arminianism was correct that he gave very little scriptural support. He appealed to the fact that the gospel is offered to all men, and that for him was enough proof that man, not God, makes the choice as to who will be saved. [12]

Unconditional Election. These religious bodies don't believe in unconditional election. The passage that is often quoted and most familiar to all is *John 3:16*. The belief is that God gave His Son to the world and not just to an elect few. This is where most Arminians *(see the Remonstrance pg. 8 #2)* hold their stance. Calvinists believe that Christ's death was sufficient for all men yet only applied to the elect. Contention about John 3:16 has provoked heated debates and caused schisms between friends and the Body of Christ. Arminians, in touting conditional election and perseverance based on man's works instead of God's finished work, removes the providential hand of God. Roman Catholics and Methodists both believe that the foreknowledge of God, in knowing how people would respond to Him, is how God chose or "elected" them.

Limited Atonement. Methodist and Catholic faiths believe Christ died for all, which is "unlimited atonement." Whereas Baptist believe that even though there is a general call *(John 3:16)*, that only few have been chosen to a more specific call *(Matt 20:16 and Matt 22:10)* this call is "limited atonement." The converse ideology of "unlimited atonement" fosters universalism, that all will be saved. What do we do when the Scriptures explicitly state that all are **not** saved, or chosen? Catholics and Methodists both have failed to answer this question successfully in regards to the *Holy Writ*.

<u>Irresistible Grace</u>. Wesleyan and Roman Catholic advocates don't believe that God's call is irresistible. Their belief is that because man's will is free, man can decide if he will choose God or not. Whereas, Baptists believe that because of God's predetermined choice, His grace makes the call overwhelming and unavoidable.

<u>Perseverance of the Saints</u>. The two Arminian-based denominations are utterly divided on this aspect. Roman Catholics base their final entrance into Heaven on their works rather than on Christ's finished work:

> Catholic dogma states: "By his good works the justified man really acquires a claim to supernatural reward from God."....Thus the Council of Trent declared that "those who work well 'unto the end' [*Mat 10:22*], and who trust in God , life eternal is to be proposed, both as a grace mercifully promised to the sons of God through Christ Jesus, 'and as a recompense' which is...to be faithfully given to their good works and merit." [13]

Whereas Methodists are more in sync with Baptists regarding merit. Roger Olsen quotes John Wesley on the matter of salvation:

> It is free in all to whom it is given. It does not depend on any power of merit in man; no, not in any degree, neither in whole, nor in part. It does not in any wise depend either on the good works

or righteousness of the receiver; not on anything he has done, or anything he is. It does not depend on his endeavors. It does not depend on his good tempers, or good desires, or good purposes and intentions; for all these flow from the free grace of God. [14]

It would seem that even though these denominations are more aligned with the Arminian views, Olson believes that just as Calvinists run the gamut of the TULIP five points; Arminians also span the points of the Remonstrance.

I too have recently learned that even within the Baptist faith, there are liberal thinkers, (not hyper or classic Calvinists). They would disregard the vast amount of Scriptures that speak to both ideals of Election and Free Will as wholly true. When I was a student at Andersonville Theological Seminary, in Camilla, GA, while studying the book of *Romans*, I was bombarded with Scriptures espousing "Free Will" from Dr. Hayes. His lectures espoused the hyper-Calvinistic view is unscriptural and that predestination is not at all what was presented in *Romans 8:29-30*. Hyper-Calvinists adhered to all five points; however, some are proponents of a four-point Calvinistic view that changes *"limited atonement"* to *"unlimited atonement."* Most Calvinists refer to the proponents as modified Arminianism. In the book Christianity According to the Bible, Ron Rhodes eloquently articulates, "Grace and meritorious works are mutually exclusive. *Romans 11:6* says this about God's salvation: *"And if by grace, then it is no longer of works; otherwise grace is no longer grace. But if it is of works, it is no longer grace; otherwise work is no longer work"* (NKJV). Gifts cannot be earned—only wages and awards can be earned." [15]

It is clear to me now, that my instructor, professing to be of the Baptist faith, was adhering to a four-point Calvinistic view. The beautiful feature about this particular seminary is that if I disagreed with the instructor's position, I was asked to defend my position as it relates to the Scriptures. When presented with the task of defending my viewpoint; I studied the Scripture references that Dr. Hayes submitted in defense against a hyper-Calvinistic view (or classical view). Additionally I searched the Scriptures to ascertain what it said about Calvin's viewpoint. After further examination of the texts and contexts, Scripture remains clear, *"all the ones in which God gave Jesus He lost none of them." (John 17:6, 9, 12).* Dr. Hayes used several Scriptures that were intended to oppose predestination and election; however, when reading the entire Scripture in context, the Scripture still supports God's selection rather than man's choice. Here are a few Scriptures taken out of context that **do not** prove his point:

- Some Arminians and four-point Calvinists believe and teach John 6:40 as if it is a stand-alone Scripture that states, it is up to man to believe only. But the preceding Scriptures say that the Father gives to the Son, and all that the Father gives won't be cast out.

- Another Scripture that these same four-point Calvinist and some Arminian Theologians use is *John 12:32* which states Jesus will draw all men unto Him; as proof that men have complete choice in the matter of salvation. This Scripture does say in fact that Jesus will draw all men unto Him, but it is not speaking of saving all men, instead it is speaking about the manner in which He will be killed (on a cruel cross): *John 12:33 This He said, signifying by what death He would die (NKJV)*. All men will be drawn to Him in the fact that this very act will be the "talk of the town" throughout the ages. God used the humiliation of the cross to glorify Himself and exalt His Son. Jesus' obedience unto death baffled the Jews; they pictured their Messiah, their King differently. For God used the cross to confound the wisest of men (*I Cor 1:20-25, 3:18-20*) and chose this act as a reconciliatory tool.

- The last example expounds on the "other crowd of Theologians" use of *John 6:29*, which emphasizes the "believe in Him" part, but haze over the Scripture about the "Work of God," not just the "believe" part. Jesus in the previous verses tells them that they are seeking Him for the wrong reason; only because their bellies are full.

However, He is the true Work of God, *"the Bread from heaven!"* Jesus continues to remind them:

John 6:35-40
"I am the bread of life. He who comes to Me shall never hunger, and he who believes in Me shall never thirst. 36 But I said to you that you have seen Me and yet do not believe. 37 All that the Father gives Me will come to Me, and the one who comes to Me I will by no means cast out. 38 For I have come down from heaven, not to do My own will, but the will of Him who sent Me. 39 This is the will of the Father who sent Me, that of all He has given Me I should lose nothing, but should raise it up at the last day. 40 And this is the will of Him who sent Me, that everyone who sees the Son and believes in Him may have everlasting life; and I will raise him up at the last day." (NKJV)

Everything starts and ends with God (John 1:3-4, *Rev 1:8*); He is the author and finisher of our faith *(Heb 12:2)*. Arminians and four-point Calvinists still have trouble refuting the whole of the Word and continue to struggle in codifying their beliefs.

Part 3

Blessed Assurance

In 1873, Frances J. Crosby, wrote these beautiful lyrics:

Blessed assurance, Jesus is mine!
Oh, what a foretaste of glory divine!
Heir of salvation, purchase of God,
Born of His Spirit, washed in His blood.

Refrain:
This is my story, this is my song, Praising my Savior all the day long;
This is my story, this is my song, Praising my Savior all the day long

"Blessed assurance, is Jesus mine?" We asked questions at the beginning of our journey about knowing God and His actual existence. Let's dig into the realm of possibility and ask, "Can we truly have blessed assurance?"

Once we know that He does exists and we get to know Him personally; does that mean this relationship extends to His Son? In this segment, we will dive deeper into the Scriptures to affirm whether they support or deny the security of salvation, election, and free will.

Isa 43:18-19

"Do not remember the former things, Nor consider the things of old. 19 Behold, I will do a new thing, Now it shall spring forth; Shall you not know it? I will even make a road in the wilderness And rivers in the desert. NKJV

Chapter 18

Salvation Security

While reading, studying, and meditating on the book of Romans; I discovered Scriptures, completed word studies in the Hebrew and Greek; and researched Soteriology. I am convinced that believers are secured in our salvation not all mankind. *Isaiah 14:12-14* shows us how Lucifer's pride introduced sin into the universe. *Romans* presented the case as to why we needed a Savior—originating with Adam's disobedience *(Rom 5:12)*. This act plagued the entire human race with being born spiritually dead with a sin-sick nature. The earth moans and groans in need of deliverance *(Rom 8:20-22)*. Elohim's (The Godhead) infinite wisdom decided in the beginning a plan and purpose for the salvation of His creation:

- The who—Elohim devised and decreed a plan for reconciliation *(II Cor 5:20-21)*
- The what and where—through the voluntary act of The Son to die on a cruel *cross (Gen 3:15)*
- The when—at the appointed time *(Isa 9:6-7, Jn 17:1-5, 18:1-20:18, Gal 4:3-5)*

- For <u>whom</u>–His election, before the foundation of the earth *(Rom 8:30)*
- The <u>why</u>–because of love *(Jn 3:16, Rom 5:8)*

God works in mysterious ways and His wonders to perform. His works are magnificent and are worthy to behold! He chooses foolish and weak things to shame the weak and mighty *(I Cor 1:27-31)*. God's plan included Him coming down through 42 generations to ensure that Jesus was in the lineage of King David and priests. David was from the tribe of Judah and priests were from the tribe of Levi. Jesus, The Christ, road upon a donkey and not upon a gallant steed; He ultimately died upon a cross. God chose the cross, which appears foolish for The Messiah and King to die this way. God would not devise this elaborate plan without an eternal purpose. Remember in chapter 10 of this book, we learned that *Romans chapter 8* began with no condemnation and ended with no separation. Once we are in Christ, absolutely nothing can separate us from Him. God the Father would not have allowed such a cruel sacrifice to be in vain. Additionally, He would not require His Son to die over and over again in such a cruel, cruel way. This would be the effect if one could lose their salvation. Under the Law, the Levitical High Priest had to make atonement (to cover) each year for Israel's sins. Christ, the Lamb of God– the perfect sacrifice, <u>took away</u> our sins <u>not just covered</u> them. He only had to do it once because He is God incarnate, The Hypostatic Union–wholly God and wholly Man!

<u>The Tenses of Salvation</u> (Chapter 14, pgs. 87-91) are an exceptional tool in helping us delineate between salvation and sanctification. Additionally, Harold L. Fickett, Jr. shares the three things that the believer can lose:

1. <u>His rewards</u>
   The believer's rewards can be lost when he does not choose to do God's will in his obedience to God *(I Cor 3:9-15)*.

2. <u>His peace</u>
   The believer can lose the peace of God, but not the peace with God. The aforementioned is aligned with sanctification while the latter is aligned with salvation

3. <u>His joy</u>
   The believer can lose the joy of his salvation when he says no to the Holy Spirit, and yes to the flesh. This is why David cried out, "Restore unto me the joy of Thy salvation, and uphold me with Thy free Spirit" *(Ps 51:12)*.
   [16]

God has assured us that if we have the Son, we have eternal life. If we have not the Son, we are condemned already *(Jn 3:17-18, I Jn 5:11-13)*. Our salvation is secure unto everlasting life and forevermore. Amen!

Rom 9:15-16, 18

For He says to Moses, "I will have mercy on whomever I will have mercy, and I will have compassion on whomever I will have compassion." 16 So then it is not of him who wills, nor of him who runs, but of God who shows mercy...18 Therefore He has mercy on whom He wills, and whom He wills He hardens. NKJV

Chapter 19

Election

In light of the material that has been shared, along with supporting Scripture references; the prevailing conclusion is: **<u>Man cannot choose to be in the Body of Christ first</u>**. God has to choose him first. Just as God chose Job, Abraham, Jacob, and Joseph, in the previous ages, He chose us for this dispensation. A primary example is the birth of a child being born into the natural world. A child can't choose or decide to be born to his parents. The parents have to act first—elect or choose to have a child. If the Arminianism position is taken, then this child-parent premise would be: the parents choose to have a child, but then the child would have to choose whether he wants to be conceived of the parents. This notion is preposterous. So if it is true in the natural, it is much truer in the spiritual realm. What God has decreed will come to pass *(Isa 55:11)*:

> *So shall My word be that goes forth from My mouth;*
> *It shall not return to Me void,*
> *But it shall accomplish what I please,*
> *And it shall prosper in the thing for which I sent it*
> *(NKJV)*

Man can't choose to be saved unless God calls him first. For there is none that are righteous, there are none who seek after God (*Ps 10:4, Rom 3:10-12*). God chooses upon who He will show mercy, and whose heart He will harden (*Rom 9:17-18*). This is the sovereignty of the Most High God. This holds fast to limited atonement.

Before the foundation of the world (which was outside of time), God chose how He would reconcile man (*Gen 3:15*), and who would be in Christ to be conformed to the image of His Son (*Rom 8:29*). When Paul said that others believed on Jesus before him; Paul was referencing the time element. Paul's manifestation of his birth in Christ in the flesh was "in time." We who are in Christ were "outside of time" which occurred before we were birthed in the flesh. God is outside of time; therefore, He sees everything in and out of time simultaneously. However, we as humans can only experience time in a linear fashion. Dimensions of time and space are very difficult for man's finite mind to comprehend. The same principle is applied in how mankind was in Adam, so all have sinned. We, the elect, were in Christ before the foundation of the world. We were chosen first, and then we were called—meaning manifested in time. Those of us who were chosen were given the ability to believe; those who weren't chosen are condemned already for unbelief (*Jn 3:16-18*). God chose which vessels would be used for honor and which for dishonor (*Rom 9:21-24*). According to

His perfect will, God hardened Pharaoh's heart and opened believers' hearts.

It was previously stated: It takes God to please God (*Rom 11:34-36, Eph 1:9, Phil 2:12-13*). Man does not have a clue how to please Him. Man, would always choose evil over good because he is innately evil because of his sin nature. The Holy Spirit, who is the third person of the Godhead, performs the convincing work on man's heart (*Jn 16:8-15*). God does the work first, and God has declared that man must respond. Free Will can't supersede election which resides in God's divine decree. God declares the end from the beginning (*Isa 46:10-11*) and we weren't there (at the beginning) to know all the intricacies of His plan. God said He chose the "*elect*" from the foundation of world. The "church" ἐκκλησία (**ĕkklēsia,** ek-klay-see´-ah), literally means, "called out ones;" His Body, not the building!

> *Eph 1:3-6*
> *Blessed be the God and Father of our Lord Jesus Christ, who has blessed us with every spiritual blessing in the heavenly places in Christ, 4 just as He chose us in Him before the foundation of the world, that we should be holy and without blame before Him in love, 5 having predestined us to adoption as sons by Jesus Christ to Himself, according to the good pleasure of His will, 6 to the praise of the glory of His grace, by which He made us accepted in the Beloved. (NKJV)*

The following tables comprise some Scriptures that Dr. Hayes presented in his lecture in support of Free Will alone versus additional Scriptures that support Election occurring beforehand. The Arminian view implies that God knew how man was going to choose; hence his Free Will was in effect first, and this is how they explain God's foreknowledge. Therefore, since man chose God first, God could now act and choose man.

Free Will Scriptures (NKJV)
(referenced by Dr. Hayes in support of Free Will)[17]

Matt 25:41
41 "Then He will also say to those on the left hand, 'Depart from Me, you cursed, into the everlasting fire prepared for the devil and his angels:

John 3:16
16 For God so loved the world that He gave His only begotten Son, that whoever believes in Him should not perish but have everlasting life.

John 12:32-33
32 And I, if I am lifted up from the earth, will draw all peoples to Myself." 33 This He said, signifying by what death He would die.

John 6:40
40 And this is the will of Him who sent Me, that everyone who sees the Son and believes in Him may have everlasting life; and I will raise him up at the last day."

John 10:7-10
Then Jesus said to them again, "Most assuredly, I say to you, I am the door of the sheep. 8 All who ever came before Me are thieves and robbers, but the sheep did not hear them. 9 I am the door. If anyone enters by Me, he will be saved, and will go in and out and find pasture.
10 The thief does not come except to steal, and to kill, and to destroy. I have come that they may have life, and that they may have it more abundantly.

Luke 19:10
10 for the Son of Man has come to seek and to save that which was lost."

John 6:29
29 Jesus answered and said to them, "This is the work of God, that you believe in Him whom He sent."

Rom 10:9-13

Free Will Scriptures (NKJV)
(referenced by Dr. Hayes in support of Free Will)[17]

9 that if you confess with your mouth the Lord Jesus and believe in your heart that God has raised Him from the dead, you will be saved. 10 For with the heart one believes unto righteousness, and with the mouth confession is made unto salvation. 11 For the Scripture says, "Whoever believes on Him will not be put to shame." 12 For there is no distinction between Jew and Greek, for the same Lord over all is rich to all who call upon Him. 13 For "whoever calls on the name of the LORD shall be saved."

Eph 1:12
12 that we who first trusted in Christ should be to the praise of His glory.

1 Tim 2:1-6
Therefore I exhort first of all that supplications, prayers, intercessions, and giving of thanks be made for all men, 2 for kings and all who are in authority, that we may lead a quiet and peaceable life in all godliness and reverence. 3 For this is good and acceptable in the sight of God our Savior, 4 who desires all men to be saved and to come to the knowledge of the truth. 5 For there is one God and one Mediator between God and men, the Man Christ Jesus, 6 who gave Himself a ransom for all, to be testified in due time, 7 for which I was appointed a preacher and an apostle — I am speaking the truth in Christ and not lying — a teacher of the Gentiles in faith and truth.

2 Peter 3:8-9
8 But, beloved, do not forget this one thing, that with the Lord one day is as a thousand years, and a thousand years as one day. 9 The Lord is not slack concerning His promise, as some count slackness, but is longsuffering toward us, not willing that any should perish but that all should come to repentance.

Election/Predestination Scriptures (NKJV)
(referenced in support of Election preceding Free Will)

John 6:44
44 No one can come to Me unless the Father who sent Me draws him;

1 Peter 2:9-10
9 But you are a chosen generation, a royal priesthood, a holy nation, His own special people, that you may proclaim the praises of Him who called you out of darkness into His marvelous light; 10 who once were not a people but are now the people of God, who had not obtained mercy but now have obtained mercy.

Rev 17:14
14 These will make war with the Lamb, and the Lamb will overcome them, for He is Lord of lords and King of kings; and those who are with Him are called, chosen, and faithful."

James 2:5
5 Listen, my beloved brethren: Has God not chosen the poor of this world to be rich in faith and heirs of the kingdom which He promised to those who love Him?

John 13:18
18 "I do not speak concerning all of you. I know whom I have chosen ; but that the Scripture may be fulfilled, 'He who eats bread with Me has lifted up his heel against Me.'

Hag 2:23
23 'In that day,' says the LORD of hosts, 'I will take you, Zerubbabel My servant, the son of Shealtiel,' says the LORD, 'and will make you like a signet ring; for I have chosen you,' says the LORD of hosts."

Matt 20:16
16 So the last will be first, and the first last. For many are called, but few chosen."

Matt 22:14
14 "For many are called, but few are chosen."

Eph 1:3-6
3 Blessed be the God and Father of our Lord Jesus Christ, who has blessed us with every spiritual blessing in the heavenly places in Christ, 4 just as He chose us in Him before the foundation of the world, that we should be holy and without blame before Him in love,

---

Election/Predestination Scriptures (NKJV)
(referenced in support of Election preceding Free Will)

---

5 having predestined us to adoption as sons by Jesus Christ to Himself, according to the good pleasure of His will, 6 to the praise of the glory of His grace, by which He made us accepted in the Beloved.

Rev 17:8
8 And those who dwell on the earth will marvel, whose names are not written in the Book of Life from the foundation of the world, when they see the beast that was, and is not, and yet is.

Rom 9:15-24
15 For He says to Moses, "I will have mercy on whomever I will have mercy, and I will have compassion on whomever I will have compassion." 16 So then it is not of him who wills, nor of him who runs, but of God who shows mercy. 17 For the Scripture says to the Pharaoh, "For this very purpose I have raised you up, that I may show My power in you, and that My name may be declared in all the earth." 18 Therefore He has mercy on whom He wills, and whom He wills He hardens. 19 You will say to me then, "Why does He still find fault? For who has resisted His will?" 20 But indeed, O man, who are you to reply against God? Will the thing formed say to him who formed it, "Why have you made me like this?" 21 Does not the potter have power over the clay, from the same lump to make one vessel for honor and another for dishonor? 22 What if God, wanting to show His wrath and to make His power known, endured with much longsuffering the vessels of wrath prepared for destruction, 23 and that He might make known the riches of His glory on the vessels of mercy, which He had prepared beforehand for glory, 24 even us whom He called, not of the Jews only, but also of the Gentiles?

Eph 1:7-12
7 In Him we have redemption through His blood, the forgiveness of sins, according to the riches of His grace 8 which He made to abound toward us in all wisdom and prudence, 9 having made known to us the mystery of His will, according to His good pleasure which He purposed in Himself, 10 that in the dispensation of the fullness of the times He might gather together in one all things in Christ, both which are in heaven and which are on earth — in Him. 11 In Him also we have obtained an inheritance, being predestined according to the purpose of Him who works all things according to the counsel of His will, 12 that we who first trusted in Christ should be to the praise of His glory.

Election/Predestination Scriptures (NKJV)
(referenced in support of Election preceding Free Will)

Eph 2:10
10 For we are His workmanship, created in Christ Jesus for good works, which God prepared beforehand that we should walk in them.

John 10:11-16
11 "I am the good shepherd. The good shepherd gives His life for the sheep. 12 But a hireling, he who is not the shepherd, one who does not own the sheep, sees the wolf coming and leaves the sheep and flees; and the wolf catches the sheep and scatters them. 13 The hireling flees because he is a hireling and does not care about the sheep. 14 I am the good shepherd; and I know My sheep, and am known by My own. 15 As the Father knows Me, even so I know the Father; and I lay down My life for the sheep. 16 And other sheep I have which are not of this fold; them also I must bring, and they will hear My voice; and there will be one flock and one shepherd.

2 Peter 3:1-7
1 Beloved, I now write to you this second epistle (in both of which I stir up your pure minds by way of reminder), 2 that you may be mindful of the words which were spoken before by the holy prophets, and of the commandment of us, the apostles of the Lord and Savior, 3 knowing this first: that scoffers will come in the last days, walking according to their own lusts, 4 and saying, "Where is the promise of His coming? For since the fathers fell asleep, all things continue as they were from the beginning of creation." 5 For this they willfully forget: that by the word of God the heavens were of old, and the earth standing out of water and in the water, 6 by which the world that then existed perished, being flooded with water. 7 But the heavens and the earth which are now preserved by the same word, are reserved for fire until the day of judgment and perdition of ungodly men.

John 6:38-40
38 For I have come down from heaven, not to do My own will, but the will of Him who sent Me. 39 This is the will of the Father who sent Me, that of all He has given Me I should lose nothing, but should raise it up at the last day. 40 And this is the will of Him who sent Me, that everyone who sees the Son and believes in Him may have everlasting life; and I will raise him up at the last day."

John 17:6-7
6 "I have manifested Your name to the men whom You have given Me out of the world. They were Yours, You gave them to Me, and they have kept Your word. 7 Now they have known that all things which You have given Me are from You.

Election/Predestination Scriptures (NKJV) (referenced in support of Election preceding Free Will)
John 17:9 9 "I pray for them. I do not pray for the world but for those whom You have given Me, for they are Yours. John 17:12 12 Those whom You gave Me I have kept; and none of them is lost... John 6:37 37 All that the Father gives Me will come to Me, and the one who comes to Me I will by no means cast out. Prov 16:4 4 The LORD has made all for Himself, Yes, even the wicked for the day of doom.

Let us now reason with one another. If classical Arminians holdfast to the belief that man can choose God prior to God choosing them, then Scripture is faulty. However, if Scripture be not faulty, then man's logic in this classical Arminian view needs revising to align with the Word of God. We know Scripture is infallible so this doctrine needs to change. Arminianism attempted to explain how Free Will works and there could be some merit in it. Nevertheless, where Scripture is silent, we must also remain silent.

Luke 4:18

"The Spirit of the LORD is upon Me, Because He has anointed Me To preach the gospel to the poor; He has sent Me to heal the broken-hearted, To proclaim liberty to the captives And recovery of sight to the blind, To set at liberty those who are oppressed; NKJV

Chapter 20

Free Will

We have engaged in a compelling comparative study of selected doctrines. We know that "Free Will" exists because the Word says so. Let us now peruse another point of view in contrast to John Wesley (and other Arminians) and Dr. Hayes (and other four-point Calvinists).

As Christians, we have often heard the faith and secular community assert that we were made in the image of God. After a closer study of the Scriptures, the truth is, Adam and Eve were made in the image of God, and the human race was made in the image of Adam. Adam and Eve's fallen nature (spiritually dead) was passed to all of the generations to come. Genesis and our cursory view of *Romans* have revealed this to us. Thus, our once true Free Will was placed in bondage after the fall, and therefore no longer free. This bondage is tied to the lie satan told Adam and Eve in the garden. They could eat of the Tree of Knowledge of Good and Evil and know good from evil; unfortunately, they would not be able to choose good over evil because of their disobedience. Their consciences were now warped, seared with a hot iron *(I Tim 4:2)*.

Initially God gave man a free will, but it had been cursed, tied-up, and tainted because of Adam's sin *(Gen 3:4-8, Rom 5:12-21)*. The first three dispensations occur between *Genesis 1:26 and Genesis 11:32* (*Innocence, Conscience, Human Government*) mirror man's spiraling nature that was outlined in *Romans' first 6 chapters*. The blood and sacrifice that were required to cover sin had to occur each year. *(See Appendix B, 157)*

Our once free will was now placed in bondage. <u>Before the world began, God planned</u> to put an impediment into the downfall of man and reconcile us back unto Himself. The first Messianic Promise in Scripture is *Gen 3:15*. This was God's decree. He planned for His elect's bounded will to become free (salvation) so that we could learn to choose Him daily (sanctification). Isaiah prophesied about this freedom in *Isaiah 61:1*:

> *"The Spirit of the Lord GOD is upon Me,*
> *Because the LORD has anointed Me*
> *To preach good tidings to the poor;*
> *He has sent Me to heal the brokenhearted,*
> *To proclaim liberty to the captives,*
> *And the opening of the prison to those who are*
> *bound;..."* (NKJV)

The ones who have not been elected still have wills, yet they are still bounded. They have the ability to choose, but will only continue to choose degrees of evil *(Rom 1:20-32)*. They will remain in this state and grow continually evil like their father, satan. With this knowledge, we gain a better understanding of how and when to use the concept of "Free Will." This explanation again debunks the Arminian view of "Free Will." Dead men don't have the ability to choose Life. However, once they have become revived, they have the capacity to choose or reject obedience to God. This is the proper progression of how "Free Will" is manifested. God initiates and requires a call and response from His people. God said, in *John 10:27-30*:

> *"...My sheep hear My voice, and I know them, and they follow Me. 28 And I give them eternal life, and they shall never perish; neither shall anyone snatch them out of My hand. 29 My Father, who has given them to Me, is greater than all; and no one is able to snatch them out of My Father's hand. 30 I and My Father are one." (NKJV)*

All those which the Father has called hear His voice and properly respond, "YES!" The convicting and convincing work of the Holy Spirit works in us and propels us to *(Jn 16:5-14)*:

- confess our sins (realize we are sinners),
- hear the Gospel and believe (realize we need a Savior)
- accept His Spirit as resident in our heart, thereby teaching us how we can choose Him. Continually learning who will sit on the seat of our heart to rule daily and each moment.

God does not force His will upon us. He is lovingly patient with us because He knows about our warring natures *(Rom 7:13-25)*. Our old man was destined to do evil, but now our new man has a free will and is no longer in bondage. We can choose to live freely *(Rom 8:14-15)*. And in doing so, the fruit of the Spirit will be manifested (Gal 5:22).

God said that He gave man "*Free Will*" *(Rom 10:13)* as His elect. The "whoever calls on the name of the Lord" is the response to His specific call: when the Holy Spirit speaks to the heart of man. It is only through this lens we see the intricacies of how Election and Free Will are both true.

Conclusion

As we come to the close of the book, this does not mean our journey has ended. I tell you that we have only just begun. The LORD has provided a plethora of Scriptures upon which to read, study and meditate. Therefore, we must continue to seek the wonderful morsels and treasures that await us in *His living Word*. Our cursory study of *Romans* cracked the door open to peruse an avalanche of Biblical gems that propel us onward in seeking truth. Tools were introduced to help us dig deeper and to properly rightly divide the *Word Of Truth*. Our *LORD is the Living Word*. He reveals and illuminates to us who He is and how we are to relinquish ourselves to Him so that He may live through us. *"Not my will, let yours be done!"*

In reading <u>Why I am a Baptist</u> edited anecdotes from several authors, I was pleased to concur with their determination that Baptist doctrines emulate Scripture. Douglas Blount emphatically concludes:

> That the Bible stands as the ultimate authority follows from the fact that it "has God for its author." Thus, Scripture carries with it the very authority of God himself. That it does so also

underlies the Baptist aversion to creeds. For the refusal to place conciliar decrees, ancient opinions, human doctrines, or private judgments above--or even on par with--Scripture results from a commitment to its divine authorship and consequent authority; such, decrees, opinions, doctrines, etc. are to be judge by—rather than to judge—the Bible. As T. T. Eaton states, "'Thus saith the Lord' is an end of all controversy." [18]

As Baptists, we believe that the Scripture is our highest authority for salvation, living, and knowledge about who God is and what He requires. It is therefore concluded that Scriptures supporting Free Will doctrine can't be used in isolation prior to salvation. Free Will Scriptures must be in concert with God's entire uncompromised Word which also includes Election. Election Scriptures can't be stand-alone concepts while ignoring Free Will. Scripture supports authenticity in both doctrines. Election for the chosen and Free Will within the believer—God not only foreknew (favored-called by name); but He also predestined (conformed to His Son) His decree. Doctrinal Scriptures illustrate emphatic beliefs but they can't explicitly prove that an unsaved man can choose God before God has chosen him. The doctrines of Salvation Security, Election, and Free Will are knitted together to form God's purpose in reconciliation. God has neither revealed His "Election selection criteria," nor if criteria even exists. Again, we didn't exist in the beginning, as God unapologetically reminded Job *(Job 38)*. The sovereign God of the Universe's Word is sure (*Psalm 19:7*) and His Word declares:

Rom 9:15-18
For He says to Moses, "I will have mercy on whomever I will have mercy, and I will have compassion on whomever I will have compassion." 16 So then it is not of him who wills, nor of him who runs, but of God who shows mercy. 17 For the Scripture says to the Pharaoh, "For this very purpose I have raised you up, that I may show My power in you, and that My name may be declared in all the earth." 18 Therefore He has mercy on whom He wills, and whom He wills He hardens. (NKJV)

and

Rom 9:20-21
But indeed, O man, who are you to reply against God? Will the thing formed say to him who formed it, "Why have you made me like this?" 21 Does not the potter have power over the clay, from the same lump to make one vessel for honor and another for dishonor? (NKJV)

For we only know in part and see things dimly (*I Cor 13:9,12*). Christians walk by faith. Just as we don't know how Jesus is both fully God and fully Man (the Hypostatic Union); or how the Holy Spirit is able to reside in a redeemed sinful man is still a part of God's mysteries. By accepting the things in which He has spoken, until we get to see Him face to face, pleases Him. This is "faith!"

These realities have valid fundamental ideas: election, eternal salvation, predestination, free will (chosen ones), and the response of obedience. We are commanded to believe the Gospel; and once it has been shared we are to share the Gospel with others. We are to win the lost (evangelize – *Rom 10:14-17*) and disciple the saved (study – *Ps 1:2, II Tim 2:15*). The Great Commission requires *(Matt 28:19-20)*, us to go preach the Gospel and to teach the new believers about all the things God has commanded.

Evangelize the lost

Matt 28:19
Go ye therefore, and teach all nations, baptizing them in the name of the Father, and of the Son, and of the Holy Ghost: (KJV)

Rom 10:14-17
How then shall they call on Him in whom they have not believed? And how shall they believe in Him of whom they have not heard? And how shall they hear without a preacher? 15 And how shall they preach unless they are sent? As it is written:
> *"How beautiful are the feet of those who preach the gospel of peace, Who bring glad tidings of good things!" 16 But they have not all obeyed the gospel. For Isaiah says, "LORD, who has believed our report?" 17 So then faith comes by hearing, and hearing by the word of God. (NKJV)*

Disciple the saved

Ps 1:2
But his delight is in the law of the LORD; and in his law doth he meditate day and night.(KJV)

Matt 28:20
20 Teaching them to observe all things whatsoever I have commanded you: and, lo, I am with you alway, even unto the end of the world. Amen. (KJV)

II Tim 2:15
Study to shew thyself approved unto God, a workman that needeth not to be ashamed, rightly dividing the word of truth. (KJV).

The late Dr. D. James Kennedy does an outstanding job in equipping churches with the tools for evangelism. In his book Evangelism Explosion, he begins with training disciples how to ascertain who they have in front of them by asking two diagnostic questions (paraphrased):

1. If you were to die tonight, do you know where you would spend eternity?
2. If God asked you, "Why should I let you into My heaven, do you know what you would say?" [19]

Dr. Kennedy does a masterful job in laying out the four possible answers to the questions, and then proceeds to show how to systematically share the Gospel using the book of Romans as an outline, with a few additional Scriptures to complete the process. Appendix D on page 179, has been shared in a succinct format to help one memorize key Scriptures to help easily share the Gospel.

I have heard from several Christians about the difficulty in sharing their testimony and the Gospel. I also wondered if there was a more pleasant and effective approach. My pastor, Sam Holmes, Jr., trained us to use this method to evangelize. Once learned, I felt freer to be utilized by the Holy Spirit in evangelistic outreach. I also began to train others to use this wonderful systematic approach. Always remember,

Proverbs 11:30 b (the verse paraphrased).

Our blessed assurance has been affirmed throughout God's Word and has been shed abroad in our hearts. Reconciliation manifests when we share the Gospel to one of His chosen. They too will hear Him call to come into the fold. In Him, we are assured that Jesus loses none who the Father gave to Him. One of my favorite assurance Scriptures is found in I John. I had no idea it was there, and must have glossed over it many times when I was younger. We call it, "The Assurance Scripture!" This Scripture will have you shouting and crying at the exact same time—knowledge is power!

I John 5:11-13
11 And this is the testimony: that God has given us eternal life, and this life is in His Son. 12 He who has the Son has life; he who does not have the Son of God does not have life.

13 These things I have written to you who believe in the name of the Son of God, that you may <u>know</u> that you have eternal life, and that you may continue to believe in the name of the Son of God. (NKJV)

We have assurance that our salvation is secure because we have been elected. We also have assurance in our sanctification process and in our glorification:

Phil 1:6
6 being confident of this very thing, that He who has begun a good work in you will complete it until the day of Jesus Christ;(NKJV)

Thank You Heavenly Father!

Jude 24-25
Now to Him who is able to keep you from stumbling,
And to present you faultless
Before the presence of His glory with exceeding joy,
25 To God our Savior,
Who alone is wise, Be glory and majesty ,
Dominion and power,
Both now and forever. Amen. (NKJV)

John 8:32 & 36

And you shall know the truth, and the truth shall make you free ."

John 8:36
Therefore if the Son makes you free , you shall be free indeed. NKJV

I Am Adopted

Verse 1
I am adopted; I'm a special kid, you see I'm proud to
be a member of the royal family my Father owns a
kingdom, and He sits upon His throne He gives me
ev'rything I need, it's nice to just belong.

Chorus
I'm adopted. I'm chosen. I bear my Father's name
just livin' the life of luxury in the castle with the King

Verse 2
I am adopted; I'm a special kid, you see there's room
in His big kingdom for a million kids like me.
He loves the little children; you're as welcome as can
be so come on up to my Father's house and join our
family.

Chorus
I'm adopted. I'm chosen. I bear my Father's name
just livin' the life of luxury in the castle with the King.
I'm adopted. I'm chosen. I bear my Father's name
just livin' the life of luxury in the castle with the King

Tag
Just livin' the life of luxury in the castle with the King

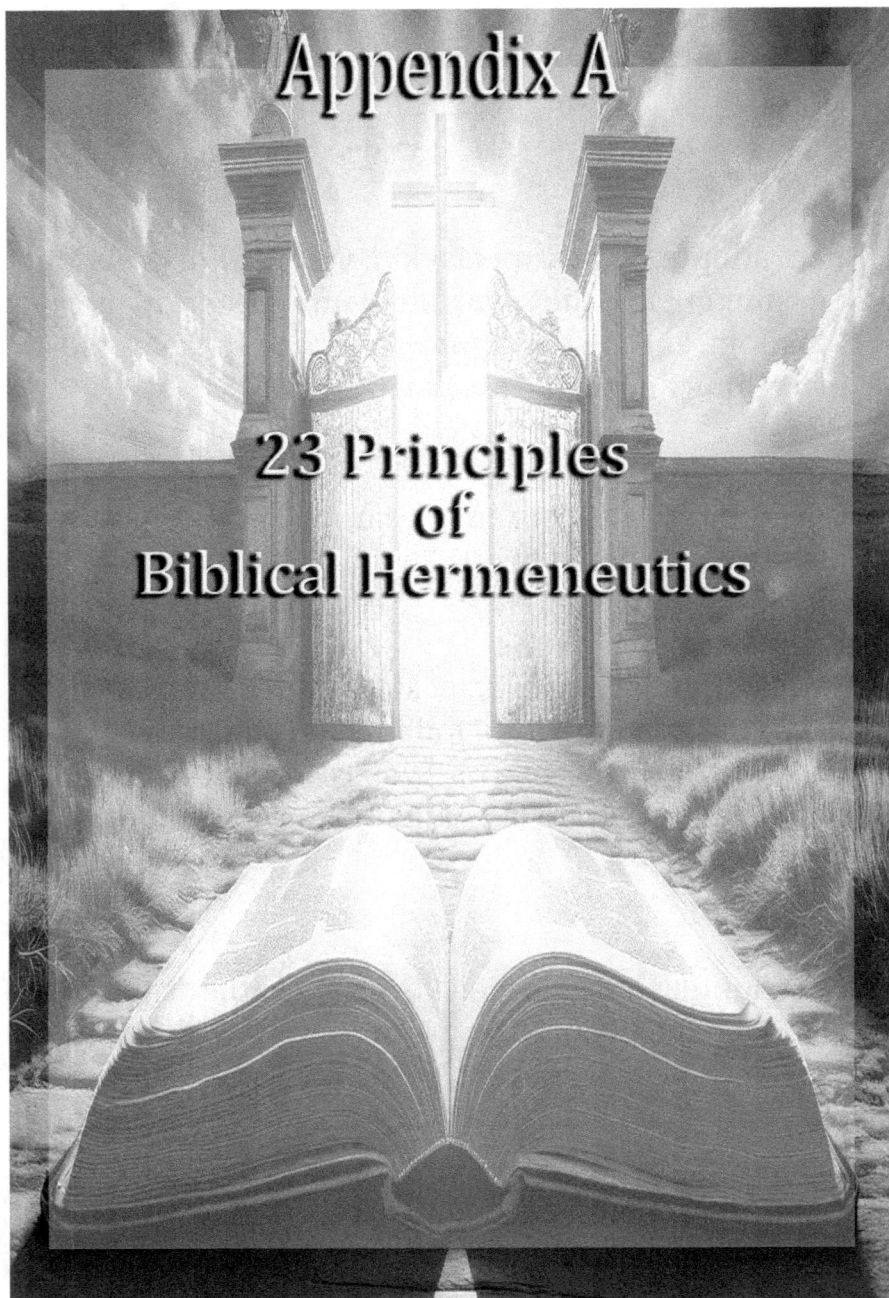

Appendix A

23 Principles of Biblical Hermeneutics

23 Principles of Biblical Hermeneutics [20]
from Principles of Biblical Hermeneutics by J. Edwin Hartill

#	Principle Name and Definition
1.	**Dispensational Principle** A dispensation is a period of time during which God deals in a particular way with man in respect to sin and man's responsibility. The word "dispensation" means "administration" and is first found in 1 Cor 9:17.

2.	**Covenantal Principle**
	An agreement or a contract between men or between men and God. Two kinds of covenants exist in the Bible:
	    1. Conditional––depends upon man.
	       Ex 19:5––"If ye will obey"––Formula
	    2. Unconditional––"I will"––Formula

3.	**Ethnic Division Principle** (pertaining to races of people)
	This is the principle by which the Word of Truth is rightly divided in relation to the three classes of which it treats, e.g., the Jew, the Gentile, and the Church.
	    1. Learn 1 Cor 10:32––"Give none offence, neither to the Jews, nor the Gentiles, nor to the Church of God."
	        a. God, while not a respecter of persons, is a respecter of classes.
	        b. Three is the number of completeness.
	            i. There are 3 in the Godhead––Father, Son, and Holy Spirit
	            ii. There are 3 places––Heaven, Earth, and Hell
	            iii. There are 3 classes––Jews, Gentiles, and Church of God.

4.	**Discrimination Principle** That principle by which we should divide the Word of Truth, so as to make distinction where God makes a difference. Failure to do this leads to confusion.
5.	**Predictive Principle** A prophet was essentially God's spokesman, and his sole

#	Principle Name and Definition
	mission was to speak the Word of God and only the words which God gave him to speak. God said to Jonah, "Go and preach what I bid thee." ...He is not only a FORETELLER, but a FORTHTELLER of the Word of God. We always think of a prophet as one who foretells the future, but primarily a prophet was not a foreteller, but he forth told the Word of God. Foretelling is only a small part of the prophet's work. A prophet is one who speaks for God, whether by way of instruction, reproof, correction, judgment, etc. A man is God's prophet when he speaks forth the Word of God. ~ There is a difference between prophecy and prediction. We have in the Bible the definition of the office and function of the prophet––Ex 7:1-c. Aaron's office as a prophet was to be the spokesman of Moses. The message of God was to come from Moses through Aaron to Pharaoh––Ex 4:15-16. Aaron was the spokesman of Moses unto the people. He was to speak the words that Moses gave him.
6.	**Application Principle** The principle by which an application may be made only after the correct interpretation has been learned.

7.	**Typical Principle**
	A type is a divinely appointed illustration of some scriptural truth.
	    1. Reasons for neglecting the study of types.
	        a. Called fanciful because of ignorance.
	            Sir Robert Anderson said, "The typology of the Old Testament is the very alphabet of the languages in which the doctrine of the New Testament is written; and as many of our great theologians are admittedly ignorant of typology, we need not feel surprised if they are not always the safest exponents of the doctrines."

#	Principle Name and Definition
	b. It is called uninteresting because difficult. This is pure laziness. The study of types takes time, work, prayer, and sweat. 2. Reason for studying types. You can never have a shadow without a body to cast that shadow. In the Old Testament you have the shadow preceding Christ, and in the New Testament you meet with the body which cast the shadow. Types are pictures or object lessons by which God taught His people concerning His grace and saving power.
8.	**Human Willingness in Illumination Principle** It is the principle by which a knowledge of God's truth is guaranteed to souls willing to know the truth——John 7:17. "If a man will to do His will," might better be translated, "He that willeth to do His will." Whatever truth a man or woman knows comes because he or she is willing to receive the truth. This has reference to the saved man. "Will"——have an absolute mind to it.

9.	**First Mention Principle**
	1. That principle by which God indicates in the first mention of a subject, the truth with which that subject stands connected in the mind of God.
	  a. Newton said, "I find in Scripture this principle of interpretation, which I believe if conscientiously adopted, will serve as an unfailing guide to what was in the mind of God. This is the keystone of the whole matter."
	  b. Dr. A.T. Pierson——"This is a law we have long since noted, and have never yet found it to fail. The first occurrence of a word, expression, or utterance, is the key to its subsequent meaning, or it will be a guide to ascertaining the essential truth connect

#	Principle Name and Definition
	with it." c. The first time a thing is mentioned in Scripture it carries with it a meaning that will be carried through the Word of God. We find 13 in Scripture used in connection with rebellion. All through Scripture 13 is a number that has in it the note of rebellion against God. It foreshadows apostasy. d. There is only one speaker throughout all Scripture, although there are many mouths. Only one providing, governing, controlling mind––Heb 1:1. God spake through "holy men of old" in the past, but in these days He speaks through His Son. No matter when, where, or how, the message is given, God is the speaker, and since there is only one speaker, and since that speaker knows from the beginning what He is going to say, He can so shape the first utterances as to forecast everything that is to follow. He is able to do that.
10.	**Progressive Mention Principle** That principle by which God makes the revelation of any given truth increasingly clear as the Word proceeds to is consummation. 1. You will find that the Word of God is a progression. As you study, it will bring added details to truth that God has revealed in the beginning. 2. There are two ways of studying Scripture: a. Canonically: in the order in which the books appear––man's order. b. Chronologically: in the order in which they were written, and the events occur––order of revelation. i. There is a teaching in the Word of God in the very arrangement of the

#	Principle Name and Definition
	books. Romans is the foundation on which all the epistles rest. Thessalonians was the first written. The Holy Spirit put it in its place in the Bible because of its teachings.
	ii. Bernard has written a book, "The Progress of Doctrine in the New Testament," in which he says, "The reality of the progression is very visible, and more especially so when we reach the New Testament––the last stages of this progressive teaching. Glance from the first words of the Bible to the last: 'In the beginning God'––'Even so, Lord Jesus.' There is a progression from one to the other. There is a difference in the rates of progress–– in the Old Testament the progress is protracted, languid, sometimes almost obscured, ending with an entire suspension for 400 years. After this, comes the New Testament and here the progress is rapid. Before, it was centuries, now it is but years. The great scheme unfolds rapidly. Just as a plan grows slowly at first and is barely visible in growth, so is the truth in the Old Testament. But in the New Testament, the plant has budded, and soon the full blossom appears. The growth then is rapid. First the root, then the shoot, and then the fruit."
	iii. The thought of progress in Scripture ought to give to us one right method

#	Principle Name and Definition
	of Bible study, and that method lies right on the surface. The Bible was written by books, and was built up by books, so it ought to be studied by books. It is a Book of books. Follow a certain subject through Scripture. You will find that it becomes complete through a steady growth. There are great highways in Scripture, and we ought to travel them just as we travel other highways. We will thus accumulate knowledge. There many speakers, but one mind.
11.	**Full Mention Principle** That principle by which God declares His full mind upon any subject vital to our spiritual life. Somewhere in the Word, God gathers together the scattered fragments that have to do with a particular truth, and puts them into one exhaustive statement. That is His full mind concerning that truth.
12.	**Context Principle** 1. That principle by which God gives light upon a subject through either near or remote passages bearing upon the same theme. Every sentence or verse in the Bible has something that precedes it and something that follows it––except Gen 1:1 and Rev 22:21. 2. Every verse must be studied in the light of its context. Never take a verse out of its setting and give it a foreign meaning.
13.	**Agreement Principle** That principle under which the truthfulness and faithfulness of God become the guarantee that He will not set forth any passage in His Word which contradicts any other passage. 1. There are no contradictions in Scripture; there is

#	Principle Name and Definition

	organic unity. Though there are 66 books, yet it is perfect unity as shown in structure, history, purpose, doctrine, and theme, which is Jesus Christ. There are always critics who declare that the Bible is full of discrepancies, inaccuracies, contradictions, and errors, but the Bible is not a Bible of mistakes, and this is guaranteed by the God of truth and faithfulness––Ps 119:90; John 17:17.
	2. If the Bible is a book of errors, then we must reach one of two conclusions.
	    a. The Bible is not God's book; for God is faithful.
	    b. If it is God's book, then God is not faithful. Both these conclusions may be rejected–– Num 23:19; Rom 3:4; Deut 32:4; Tit @:2. There are a lot of books written by man which do not contain the truth, and many commentaries on Scripture do not contain it. God is the Author of the Bible, through the Holy Spirit, and the Bible is a perfect unity, though ridiculed by many modernists.

14.	**Direct Statement Principle** The principle under which God says what He means, and means what He says.
15.	**Gap Principle** That principle of divine revelation whereby God in the Jewish Scriptures ignores certain periods of time, leaping over centuries without comment. This is a principle that is not recognized by all Bible teachers and students.
16.	**Three-fold Principle** The principle of Bible study in which God sets forth the truths of salvation in a three-fold way; past-justification; present-transformation; future-consummation. 1. This principle expresses the grace of God and shows the fullness, completeness, and richness of

#	Principle Name and Definition

	our eternal salvation. It is found all the way through the Word of God.
	
	2. This three-fold principle meets the three pre-eminent needs of man:
	   a. Salvation from the wrath of God––Rom 1:18; 2:23; John 3:36.
	   b. Salvation from the bondage of sin––Rom 7:15.
	   c. Salvation from the physical distress, disease, death, and decay––Rom 6:23.
	
	3. Every misery and woe of the human race springs from these three conditions of man:
	   a. Separation of the soul from God.
	   b. Slavery in the bondage of sin.
	   c. The mortal and infirm condition of the body.
	
	4. Sin has brought on us:
	   a. Damned souls.
	   b. Sin-blighted lives.
	   c. Death and decay-doomed bodies.
	
	5. God provides for three pre-eminent needs of man in his three-fold plan of salvation. Salvation is something past, something present, and something future. Every Bible student will agree that this is found in the Word of God. The Christian's only foundation is the finished work of Christ.
	   a. Past––Justification, which gives man a ground for the hope that is within him.
	   b. Present––This aspect is manifested in the daily walk of the Christian who should so live and walk as to honor God. This is possible, not because of what we are in ourselves, but because of the indwelling Holy Spirit.

#	Principle Name and Definition

	6. Man is saved from the:
	   a. Penalty of sin,
	     This is past, and has to do with the wrath of God. "He was wounded for our transgressions" that we might not be wounded. God laid our sin on Him.
	   b. Power of sin,
	     Salvation from the habit of sin and the bondage of son, in this present day. Whenever a Christian is given over to fleshly desires and appetites he does not have fellowship with God, and does not have victory. His life is powerless and barren. No life that is filled with fleshly desires and worldly activities is ever fruitful.
	   c. The Presence of sin
	     When this salvation has reached its consummation, we will be given not only a redeemed soul and spirit, but also a redeemed body. Some people think that if you have enough faith you will not have bodily ills; but immortality will not come until Christ returns.
	7. Man could not meet these needs in his own strength.
	   a. God knows that man could not get right with God, so God laid the foundation for this remedy in the cross.
	   b. God knows that man is too sinful and weak to live aright, so He bestowed upon us the Holy Spirit, and has given Jesus Christ a place in heaven as our intercessor and advocate.
	   c. God knows that man cannot get out of the grave, nor give himself a new body, so God provided the resurrection; or rejuvenation,

#	Principle Name and Definition
	as the case may be.

17.	**Election Principle**
	That principle of divine revelation whereby God in working out His purposes set aside all firsts and established all seconds.
	    1. God has a purpose and this is worked out all through Scripture.
	    2. For example: Rom 9:10-12. The purpose of God declared that the elder should serve the younger; and nothing can set this aside. It is clear and candid. The seconds that the Lord establishes are established on the basis of the cross.
	    3. The reason why God sets aside the firsts is because the firsts are of the flesh and of Satan; and the seconds are associated with the spiritual and with the Lord Jesus Christ.

18.	**Repetition Principle** That principle under which God repeats some truth or subject already given, generally with the addition of details not before given. This principle is closely allied to the progressive mention principle. "Repetitions with additions." Repetitions are made for the sake of additional information.
19.	**Synthetic Principle** That principle under which God superintends the literary structure of the Bible so that it is construed in introversion, alternations, or combination of both.

20	**Illustrative Mention Principle**
	It is that principle by which God exhibits by illustrations of judgment, His displeasure at various forms of sin and disobedience.
	    1. He speaks by way of judgment for violation of His command. He gives a decisive sign of hatred of sin and then is silent for a long time.
	    2. If God visited every sin with deserved punishment as soon as a law was broken, the human race

#	Principle Name and Definition
	would soon become extinct.
21.	**Double Reference Principle** It is that peculiarity of the writing of the Holy Spirit, by which a passage applying primarily to a person or event near at hand, used by him at a later time as applying to the Peron of Christ, or the affairs of His kingdom. Human writers may not have had this in mind, but the Spirit knew.
22	**Christo-Centric Principle** It is that principle by which God shows: 1. The mind of Deity is eternally centered in Christ. 2. All angelic thought and ministry are centered in Christ. 3. All Satanic hatred and subtlety are centered at Christ. 4. All human hopes are, and human occupations should be centered in Christ. 5. The whole material universe in creation is centered in Christ. 6. The entire written Word is centered in Christ.
23	**Numerical Principle** Someone has truly said, "Strengthening to the believer's heart is the subject of Spiritual arithmetic, as revealed in God's Word." Such a subject that One Supreme Mind must have been the author of all the books of the Bible. The number ONE is a primary number. All other numbers depend upon ONE. It precedes and produces all other numbers; that is, every digit is dependent upon number ONE.

1 Jn 2:15-16

Do not love the world or the things in the world. If anyone loves the world, the love of the Father is not in him. 16 For all that is in the world — the lust of the flesh, the lust of the eyes, and the pride of life — is not of the Father but is of the world. NKJV

Appendix B

Dispensations

DISPENSATIONS

A dispensation is, the way in which God chooses to deal with man during a particular period of time to show man that he cannot be made righteous apart from Him.

The Bible is divided into7 dispensations:

I.   The Dispensation of Innocence

A. The corresponding covenant: <u>EDENIC</u> – made with Adam and Eve in Eden.

B. The Scripture Portion: Gen 1:26 – 3:24

C. Duration: Time unknown – Creation to Expulsion.

D. Man's condition: Innocent, not righteous
   1. Created in God's image (moral nature) – Gen 1:26,27
   2. Placed in a perfect environment – Gen 2:9-15
   3. Provided with abundant food – Gen 1:29; 2:9,16

E. Governmental test: Recognized God's authority. Gen 2:17

F. Man's Failure:
   1. Satan's method. Gen 3:1-5
      a. Doubt God's Word – "hath God said..." – Gen 3:1
      b. Deny God's judgment – "ye shall not surely die..." – Gen 3:4
      c. Deify man – "ye shall be as gods." – Gen 3:5
   2. Satan's appeal. Gen 3:6
      a. Lust of the flesh – "good for food."
      b. Lust of the eye – "pleasant to the eyes."
      c. Pride of life – "desired to make one wise."
   3. Eve's response. Gen 3:6

          a. She took.
          b. She ate.
          c. She gave.
    4. The immediate results. Gen 3:7
    5. The forced confession. Gen 3:8-10

G.   God's judgment: Gen 3:14-24
      N.B. The following were affected:
        1. Satan – 14,15
        2. Woman – 16
        3. Man – 17-19
        4. The ground 17

H.   Salvation requirements:
        1. Blood – Heb 9:22 – cf. coats of skin – Gen 3:21
        2. Faith – Heb 11:6 – cf. called wife Eve – Gen 3:20

I. God's gracious provision: Gen 3:15, 21,24
    1. The promise of the redeemer – Gen 3:15
    2. The protection of His righteousness – Gen 3:21
    3. The invitation to His altar – Gen 3:24

J. Christ is seen: Gen 3:31 – the coats of skin, cf. Rom 3:22, II Cor 5:21, Rev 19:8

II.   The Dispensation of Conscience

A. The corresponding covenant: <u>ADAMIC</u>.

B. The Scripture Portion: Gen 4:1 – 8:19

C. Duration: c 1600 years – from the fall to the flood.

D. Man's condition:
    1. Possessed conscience, i.e. with knowledge of right

        and wrong.
    2. Possessed information about sacrifice – Gen 4:3,4

E. Governmental test:
    1. Performed what he knew to be right.
    2. Left conscience without God's detailed revelation.

F. Man's Failure:
    1. Substitute work of his hands for the blood of the Lamb. Gen 4:13. A common present-day practice.
    2. Spurns God's gracious appeal to correct his mistake. Gen 4:7
    3. Commits murder. Gen 4:8
    4. Moral corruption through intermarriage with spirit beings. Gen 6:2,4
    5. Wickedness increased. Note development in verses 5 & 11.
    6. Noah was the exception, the faithful remnant.

G. God's judgment: Gen 7:23 – the universal flood.

H. Salvation requirements:
    1. Blood – Abel's lamb – Gen 4:4
    2. Faith – Abel's faith – Gen 4:8 cf. Heb 11:4

I. God's gracious provision: Gen 7:1
    1. Noah was patient in preaching.
    2. Noah prepared for his house – Heb 11:7, cf, Acts 15:31
    Note: "Come thou, head of the house, come first"
    3. Noah was preserved through judgment.

J. Christ is seen: Our Protection from judgment.
    1. Ark "pitched;" word translated "atonement." – Lev 17:11
    2. God shut the door – Gen 7:16 cf. John 10:28-30

III. The Dispensation of Human Government

A. The corresponding covenant: <u>NOAHIC</u>.

B. The Scripture Portion: Gen 8:20 – 11:32

C. Duration: c 400 years –the flood To Babel.

D. Man's condition: Eight persons only, under five distinct revelations
   1. Dominion ever creations confirmed – Gen 9:2 cf. Gen 1:26
   2. The flesh of animals to be used for food – Gen 9:3 cf. Gen 1:29-30
   3. Assured that the order of seasons would continue – Gen 8:22
   4. No more universal destruction of life by water – Gen 8:21, 9:11
   5. The prophecy regarding Shem, Ham, and Japheth's descendants – Gen 9:26-27

E. Governmental test:
   1. The responsibility for human government – Gen   9:5,6
      Note: Capital punishment the basic principle of all government – Gen 9:6
   2. The responsibility to re-people the earth – Gen 9:1,7

F. Man's Failure:
   1. The drunkenness of Noah – Gen 9:21
   2. Established an universal religious brotherhood – Gen 11:4
   3. Disobeyed God's command to spread abroad – Gen 11:4
   4. Consider the failure of all human governments – Gen 11:6-8 cf. Dan 2:38-44; 2:21; 4:17, 25, 32; Rev 17:17

G.   God's judgment: Tower of Babel; confusion of tongues. Present day language and nations the result – Gen 11:5-8

H.   Salvation requirements:
        1. Blood – Noah's altar – Gen 8:2
        2. Faith – Noah's offering – Gen 8:20

I.   God's gracious provision: He provided for Abraham through Shem – Gen 11:10-26, cf. Gal 3:8, 14,16, 29

J.   Christ is seen: Noah's burnt offering – Gen 8:20
        1. Ark "pitched;" word translated "atonement." – Lev 17:11
        2. God shut the door – Gen 7:16 cf. John 10:28-30

IV. The Dispensation of Promise

A. The corresponding covenant: <u>ABRAHAMIC</u>.
        1. Unconditional – all promises have been or will be fulfilled.
        2. Confirmed:
            a. To Abraham – Gen 12:14-18; 15:1-21; 17:1-19; 22:15-18
            b. To Isaac – Gen 26:1-5
            c. To Jacob – Gen 28:1-14; 35:11,12

B. The Scripture Portion: Gen 12:1 – Ex 18:27

C. Duration: c 600 years – Call of Abraham to Sinai.
        1. God's everlasting covenant with Abraham continued after man's failure
        2. Israel lost blessing, but <u>not</u> her covenant – Jer 31:35-37; Ezek 39:23-29

D. Man's condition:

    1. Abraham called out of Ur of the Chaldees
    2. Abraham given the seven-fold covenant – Gen 12:1-3

E. Governmental test: Enter into Canaan <u>and remain there</u> – Gen 12:1; 26:1-4
   Note: Egypt is a type of the world

F. Man's Failure:
    1. Abraham in Egypt – Gen 12:10
    2. Abraham in Gerar – Gen 20:1
    3. Isaac in Gerar – Gen 26:1-6, 17
    4. Isaac in Egypt – Gen 47:11

G. God's judgment: The Egyptian bondage – Ex 1:7-14

H. Salvation requirements:
    1. Blood – Abraham altar – Gen 12:7, 8, cf. Heb 9:22
    2. Faith – Abraham's faith – Rom 4:3, cf. Heb 11:6

I. God's gracious provision: Deliverance provided through Moses – Ex 3:1-10; 14:29-31

J. Christ is seen: Noah's burnt offering – Gen 8:20
    1. Offering of Isaac – Gen 22
    2. Passover Lamb – Ex 12

V.   The Dispensation of Law

A. The corresponding covenant: <u>MOSAIC</u>.

B. The Scripture Portion: Ex 19:1; Matt 27:50

C. Duration: c 1500 years –Sinai to Calvary

D. Man's condition:
    1. Law given to the nation of Israel – Ex 19:1, 3, 5, 6; 20:2, cf. Rom 2:14

Duet 4:1; 5:1; 6:3,4
2. Law proposed, accepted, then imposed – cf. Deut 19:4, 5, 6; 20:3-5

E. Governmental test:
    1. Observe to do all the law demanded – Deut 5:1; Rom 10:5
    2. Three divisions of law:
        a. Commandments – Ex 20:1-17
        b. Civil – Ex 21:; 23:33
        c. Ceremonial – Ex 25:1; 40:38
    3. Salvation impossible under law – Gal 2:16; 21; 3:11, 13, 19, 24, 25

F. Man's Failure: cf. Ex 23; 32:1-4; Acts 7:51-53

G. God's judgment:
    1. Assyrian captivity for Israel – II Kings 17:7-23
    2. Babylonian captivity for Judah – II Chron 36:15-21
    3. World-wide dispersion – Luke 21: 24

H. Salvation requirements:
    1. Blood – Heb 9:22, Lev 17:11
    2. Faith – Heb 11:6, Lev 16:21,22

I. God's gracious provision: Tabernacle, God's dwelling place – Ex 40:33-38

J. Christ is seen:
    1. Burnt offering – Lev 1
    2. Meat offering – Lev 2
    3. Peace offering – Lev 3
    4. Sin offering – Lev 4
    5. Trespass offering – Lev 5

VI. The Dispensation of Grace

A. The corresponding covenant: <u>ABRAHAMIC-New Covenant</u>.
    1. Abrahamic – Gal 3:7-9, 14, 29 (read carefully)

2. New Covenant – Matt 26:28; I Cor 11:25
   a. Called "new" as related to old (Mosaic) covenant
   b. New Covenant primarily for Israel – Jer 31:31-34; 32:37-41; Heb 8:8-13
   c. We Gentiles share in spiritual blessings I Cor 10:16,17; Luke 22:20

B. The Scripture Portion: Acts 2:1; Rev 19:11-16

C. Duration: ? years – Pentecost to the Revelation

D. Man's condition:
   1. Both Jews and Gentiles crucified Christ – Acts 4:27
   2. All Jews and Gentiles under sin – Rom 3:9, 15:12; Gal 3:22
   3. Only way of Salvation for both Jews and Gentiles – Acts 4:12, 15:11

E. Governmental test:
   1. Believe the record concerning God's Son – John 20:31; I John 5:9-13; II Tim 3:15
   2. Receive Christ as personal Savior – John 1:12, 3:18,36
   3. Make Christ known to the whole world – Acts 1:8; II Cor 5:17-20

F. Man's Failure:
   1. Church will be completed – Matt 16:18; Acts 14:14-16; Rom 11:25
   2. Humanity will fall – I Tim 4:1-3; II Tim 3:1-7
   3. Individual Christians will fail to evangelize the world

G. God's judgment: The Great Tribulation – Rev 4 – 19

H. Salvation requirements:
   1. Blood – Heb 9:22, I Peter 1:18,19

2. Faith – Heb 11:6, Eph 2:8

I. God's gracious provision:
    1. Whosoever will may come – John 3:16, 6:3
    2. Pre-tribulation rapture – I Thes 4:16,17

J. Christ is seen: Luke 24:27, 32; John 16:13,14; II Cor 3:18, 5:7

**THE RAPTURE HAPPENS THEN
TRIBULATION PERIOD OCCURS HERE AND
LASTS FOR 7 YEARS.
It is broken up into 2 distinct parts:
1. The Tribulation and (3.5 yrs)
2. The Great Tribulation (3.5 yrs)***

VII. The Dispensation of the Kingdom

A. The corresponding covenants: <u>ABRAHAMIC, DAVIC, PALESTINIAN, NEW COVENANT.</u>
    1. Abrahamic – Gal 3:7-9, 14, 29 (read carefully)
        a. Gen 12:1-3
        b. Gen 13:14-27
        c. Gen 15:18-21
        d. Gen 17
    2. Davidic – II Sam 7:8-16, a house (family), a throne, a Kingdom forever
    3. Palestinian
        a. Duet 28:64-67 Dispersion
        b. Duet 30:2   Repentance
        c. Duet 30:3-5   Restoration
        d. Duet 30:6   Conversion
        e. Duet 30:9   Prosperity
    4. New Covenant – Jer 31:31-38, 32:37-41, 50:4,5

B. The Scripture Portion: Rev 19:11 – 21:1 (See Prophets, Matthew, Rev, etc.)

C. Duration: 1000 years – Revelation to the New Heaven and New Earth

D. Man's condition:
   1. All enter the Kingdom saved:
      a. Believers caught up at the rapture – I Thes 4:17
      b. Enemies judged at the revelation – II Thes 1:6-10
      c. Nation of Israel converted – Zech 12:1 – 13:1
   2. Present Day conditions greatly altered:
      a. Satan is bound – Rev 20:1-3
      b. Israel is restored to leadership – Duet 28:13; Isa 66:8
      c. Creation restored to Edenic conditions – Isa 35
      d. Christ established on throne of David – Ps 2:6; Isa 11:1,9
      e. Universal peace prevails – Isa 2:2-4; Micah 4:1-5

E. Governmental test:
   1. Christ present personally – Rev 19:16, 20:6; Zech 14:9
   2. Christ enforces His law from Zion
   3. Christ demands obedience and worship – Ps 86:9; Isa 12:4-6; Zech 14:16-19

F. Man's Failure:
   1. Satan loosed for a season – Rev 20:7
   2. Man joins Satan to dethrone Christ – Rev 20:8,9

G. *God's judgment: The Great Tribulation – Rev 4 – 19
   1. Satan's armies destroyed by fire – Rev 20:9
   2. The final doom of Satan – Rev 20:10
   3. Unbelievers of all ages judged – Rev 20:11-15 *(Great White Throne Judgment)*

H. Salvation requirements:
    1. Blood – Heb 9:22, Ezek 43:19-27
    2. Faith – Heb 11:6, Isa 12:-2

I. God's gracious provision: come – Rev 21:1-5

J. Christ is seen:
    1. King of Kings – Rev 19:16
    2. The Great Judge – Rev 20:11

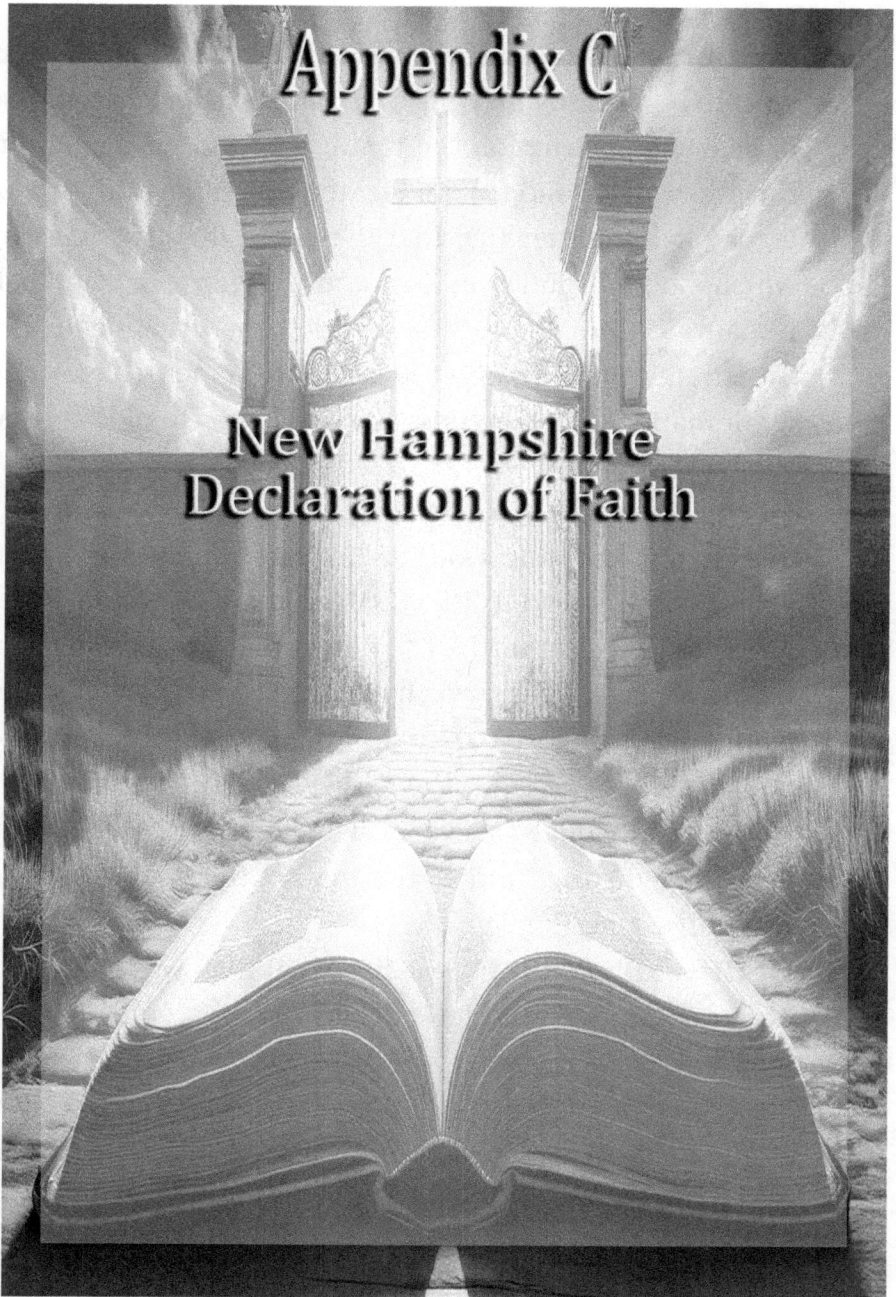

Appendix C

New Hampshire Declaration of Faith

The Confession stated:

1. **Of the Scriptures.** We believe that the Holy Bible was written by men divinely inspired, and is a perfect treasure of heavenly instruction (1); that it has God for its author, salvation for its end (2), and truth without any mixture of error for its matter (3); that it reveals the principles by which God will judge us (4); and therefore is, and shall remain to the end of the world, the true center of Christian union (5), and the supreme standard by which all human conduct, creeds, and opinions should be tried (6).

2. **Of the True God.** We believe that there is one, and only one, living and true God, an infinite, intelligent Spirit, whose name is JEHOVAH, the Maker and Supreme Ruler of Heaven and earth (7); inexpressibly glorious in holiness (8), and worthy of all possible honor, confidence, and love (9); that in the unity of the Godhead there are three persons, the Father, the Son, and the Holy Ghost (10); equal in every divine perfection (11), and executing distinct and harmonious offices in the great work of redemption (12).

3. **Of the Fall of Man.** We believe that man was created in holiness, under the law of his Maker (13); but by voluntary transgression fell from that holy and happy state (14); in consequence of which all mankind are now sinners (15), not by constraint, but choice (16); being by nature utterly void of that holiness required by the law of God, positively inclined to evil; and therefore under just

condemnation to eternal ruin (17), without defense or excuse (18).

4. **Of the Way of Salvation.** We believe that the salvation of sinners is wholly of grace (19), through the mediatorial offices of the Son of God (20); who by the appointment of the Father, freely took upon him our nature, yet without sin (21); honored the divine law by his personal obedience (22), and by his death made a full atonement for our sins (23); that having risen from the death, he is now enthroned in heaven (24); and uniting in his wonderful person the tenderest sympathies with divine perfections, he is every way qualified to be a suitable, a compassionate, and an all- sufficient Savior (25).

5. **Of Justification.** We believe that the great gospel blessing which Christ (26) secures to such as believe in him is Justification (27); that Justification includes the pardon of sin (28), and the promise of eternal life on principles of righteousness (29); that it is bestowed, not in consideration of any works of righteousness which we have done, but solely through faith in the Redeemer's blood (30); by virtue of which faith his perfect righteousness is freely imputed to us of God (31); that it brings us into a state of most blessed peace and favor with God, and secures every other blessing needful for time and eternity (32).

6. **Of the Freeness of Salvation.** We believe that the blessings of salvation are made free to all by the gospel (33); that it is the immediate duty of all to accept them by a cordial, penitent, and obedient faith (34); and that nothing prevents the salvation of the greatest sinner on

earth but his own inherent depravity and voluntary rejection of the gospel (35); which rejection involves him in an aggravated condemnation (36).

7. **Of Grace in Regeneration.** We believe that, in order to be saved, sinners must be regenerated, or born again (37); that regeneration consists in giving a holy disposition to the mind (38); that it is effected in a manner above our comprehension by the power of the Holy Spirit, in connection with divine truth (39), so as to secure our voluntary obedience to the gospel (40); and that its proper evidence appears in the holy fruits of repentance, and faith, and newness of life (41).

8. **Of Repentance and Faith.** We believe that Repentance and Faith are sacred duties, and also inseparable graces, wrought in our souls by the regenerating Spirit of God (42); whereby being deeply convinced of our guilt, danger, and helplessness, and of the way of salvation by Christ (43), we turn to God with unfeigned contrition, confession, and supplication for mercy (44); at the same time heartily receiving the Lord Jesus Christ as our Prophet, Priest, and King, and relying on him alone as the only and all-sufficient Savior (45).

9. **Of God's Purpose of Grace.** We believe that Election is the eternal purpose of God, according to which he graciously regenerates, sanctifies, and saves sinners (46); that being perfectly consistent with the free agency of man, it comprehends all the means in connection with the end (47); that it is a most glorious display of God's sovereign goodness, being infinitely free, wise, holy, and unchangeable (48); that it utterly excludes boasting, and

promotes humility, love, prayer, praise, trust in God, and active imitation of his free mercy (49); that it encourages the use of means in the highest degree (50); that it may be ascertained by its effects in all who truly believe the gospel (51); that it is the foundation of Christian assurance (52); and that to ascertain it with regard to ourselves demands and deserves the utmost diligence (53).

10. **Of Sanctification.** We believe that Sanctification is the process by which, according to the will of God, we are made partakers of his holiness (54); that it is a progressive work (55); that it is begun in regeneration (56); and that it is carried on in the hearts of believers by the presence and power of the Holy Spirit, the Sealer and Comforter, in the continual use of the appointed means-- especially the Word of God, self-examination, self-denial, watchfulness, and prayer (57).

11. **Of the Perseverance of Saints.** We believe that such only are real believers as endure unto the end (58); that their persevering attachment to Christ is the grand mark which distinguishes them from superficial professors (59); that a special Providence watches over their welfare (60); and they are kept by the power of God through faith unto salvation (61).

12. **Of the Harmony of the Law and the Gospel.** We believe that the Law of God is the eternal and unchangeable rule of his moral government (62); that it is holy, just, and good (63); and that the inability which the Scriptures ascribe to fallen men to fulfill its precepts arises entirely from their love of sin (64); to deliver them

from which, and to restore them through a Mediator to unfeigned obedience to the holy Law, is one great end of the Gospel, and of the means of grace connected with the establishment of the visible Church (65).

13. **Of a Gospel Church.** We believe that a visible Church of Christ is a congregation of baptized believers (66), associated by covenant in the faith and fellowship of the gospel (67); observing the ordinances of Christ (68); governed by his laws (69), and exercising the gifts, rights, and privileges invested in them by his Word (70); that its only scriptural officers are Bishops, or Pastors, and Deacons (71), whose qualifications, claims, and duties are defined in the Epistles to Timothy and Titus.

14. **Of Baptism and the Lord's Supper.** We believe that Christian Baptism is the immersion in water of a believer (72), into the name of the Father, and Son, and Holy Ghost (73); to show forth, in a solemn and beautiful emblem, our faith in the crucified, buried, and risen Saviour, with its effect in our death to sin and resurrection to a new life (74); that it is prerequisite to the privileges of a Church relation; and to the Lord's Supper (75), in which the members of the Church, by the sacred use of bread and wine, are to commemorate together the dying love of Christ (76); preceded always by solemn self- examination (77).

15. **Of the Christian Sabbath.** We believe that the first day of the week is the Lord's Day, or Christian Sabbath (78); and is to be kept sacred to religious purposes (79), by abstaining from all secular labor and sinful recreations (80); by the devout observance of all the means of grace,

both private (81) and public (82); and by preparation for that rest that remaineth for the people of God (83).

16. **Of Civil Government.** We believe that civil government is of divine appointment, for the interests and good order of human society (84); and that magistrates are to be prayed for, conscientiously honored and obeyed (85); except only in things opposed to the will of our Lord Jesus Christ (86) who is the only Lord of the conscience, and the Prince of the kings of the earth (87).

17. **Of the Righteous and the Wicked.** We believe that there is a radical and essential difference between the righteous and the wicked (88); that such only as through faith are justified in the name of the Lord Jesus, and sanctified by the Spirit of our God, are truly righteous in his esteem (89); while all such as continue in impenitence and unbelief are in his sight wicked, and under the curse (90); and this distinction holds among men both in and after death (91). 18. Of the World to Come We believe that the end of the world is approaching (92); that at the last day Christ will descend from heaven (93), and raise the dead from the grave to final retribution (94); that a solemn separation will then take place (95); that the wicked will be adjudged to endless punishment, and the righteous to endless joy (96); and that this judgment will fix forever the final state of men in heaven or hell, on principles of righteousness (97).

18. **Of the World to Come.** We believe that the end of the world is approaching; that at the last day Christ will descend from heaven, and raise the dead from the grave to final retribution; that a solemn separation will then

take place; that the wicked will be adjudged to endless punishment, and the righteous to endless joy; and that this judgment will fix forever the final state of men in heaven or hell, or principles of righteousness.

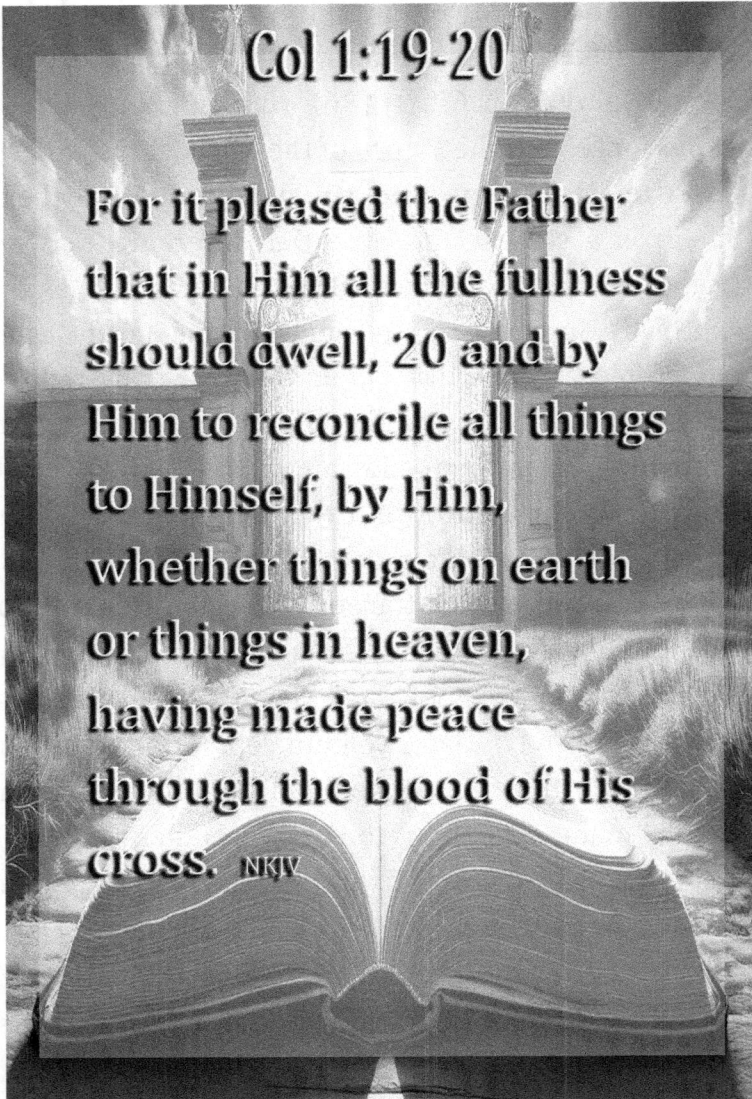

Col 1:19-20

For it pleased the Father that in Him all the fullness should dwell, 20 and by Him to reconcile all things to Himself, by Him, whether things on earth or things in heaven, having made peace through the blood of His cross. NKJV

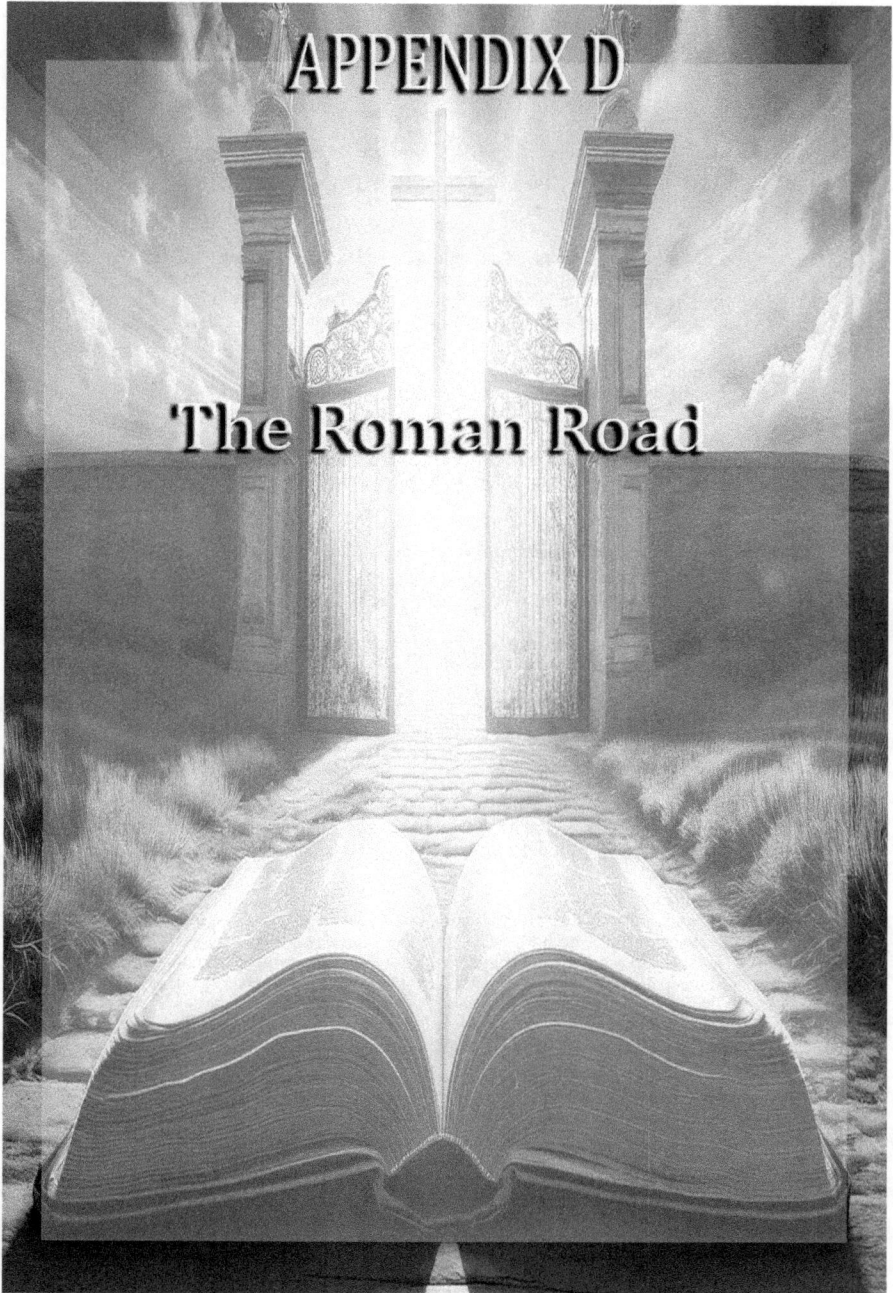

APPENDIX D

The Roman Road

If you died tonight, do you know where you would spend eternity?

If you died tonight and God asked you why should He let you into His heaven, what would your answer be?

Ephesians2:8-10
8 For by grace are ye saved through faith; and that not of yourselves: it is the **gift of God**:9 Not of works, lest any man should boast. 10 For we are his workmanship, created in Christ Jesus unto good works that God has before ordained that we should walk in them.

Romans 3:23
For **all have sinned**, and come short of the glory of God;

Romans 5:12
Wherefore, as **by one man sin entered into the world**, and death by sin; and so death passed upon all men, for that all have sinned:

Romans 6:23
For the **wages of sin is death**; but the gift of God is eternal life through Jesus Christ our Lord.

Romans 5:8
But God commendeth **his love** toward us, in that, while we were yet sinners, Christ died for us.

Hebrews 9:27
And it is **appointed unto men once to die**, but after this the judgment:

I Corinthians 15:3-4
3 For I delivered unto you first of all that which I also received, how that **Christ died for our sins** according to the scriptures; 4 And that **he was buried**, and that **he rose again** the third day according to the scriptures.

Romans 10:9-13
9 That if thou shalt **confess** with thy mouth the Lord Jesus, and shalt **believe** in thine heart **that God hath raised him from the dead**, thou shalt be saved. 10 For with the heart man believeth unto righteousness; and with the mouth confession is made unto salvation. 11 For the scripture saith, "Whosoever believeth on him shall not be ashamed." 12 For there is no difference between the Jew and the Greek: for the same Lord over all is rich unto all that call upon him. 13 For whosoever shall call upon the name of the Lord shall be saved.

I John 5:11-13
11And this is the record, that God hath given to us **eternal life**, and **this life is in his Son**. 12He that hath the Son hath life; and he that hath not the Son of God hath not life. 13These things have I written unto you that believe on the name of the Son of God; that ye may know that ye have eternal life, and that ye may believe on the name of the Son of God.

"...he who is wise wins souls." Proverbs 11:30 b

ENDNOTES

1. Wayne Grudem, Systematic Theology, 21.

2. E.Y. Mullins, Baptist Beliefs, "New Hampshire Declaration of Faith."

3. Erwin Lutzer, The Doctrines That Divide, 196-197.

4. Various., The MacArthur Lifeworks Library/Libronix Digital Library System, G4102.

5. Harold L. Fickett, Jr., A Layman's Guide to Baptist Beliefs, 127.

6. Lewis Sperry Chafer, Major Bible Themes, 230.

7. Chad Owen Brand, editor; Perspectives, 72.

8. Roger E. Olson, Arminian Theology, Myths and Realities, 32.

9. Olson, 17.

10. Dennis Bratcher, TULIP acrostic, crivoice.org /tulip.html.

11. Norman L Geisler, Roman Catholics and Evangelicals, 177.

12. Lutzer, 203.

13. Geisler, 227.

14. Olsen, 188.

15. Ron Rhodes, Christianity According to the Bible, 135.

16. Fickett, 130.

17. Dr. Jimmy Hayes, <u>Election vs Free Will; Can Salvation Be Lost</u>,

18. Tom J Nettles, editor; <u>Why I am a Baptist</u>, 177.

19. Dr. D. James Kennedy, <u>Evangelism Explosion,</u> 31.

20. J. Edwin Hartill, <u>Principles of Biblical Hermeneutics</u>, 143.

BIBLIOGRAPHY

God, Jesus, The Holy Spirit; The Holy Bible; KJV, NKJV, NASB, GREEK

Beverly, James A.; Nelson's Illustrated Guide to Religions; Nelson, TN; © 2009.

Brand, Chad Owen, editor; Perspectives; B&H, TN; © 2006.

Bratcher, Dennis, TULIP Acrostic, © 2018.

Chafer, Lewis Sperry; Major Bible Themes; Zondervan, MI; © 1974.

Fickett, Harold L.; A Layman's Guide to Baptist Beliefs; Zondervan, MI; © 1965.

Geisler, Norman L; Roman Catholics and Evangelicals; BakerBooks, MI; © 1995.

Grudem, Wayne L.; Systematic Theology; Zondervan, MI; © 2000.

Libronix; Digital Library System; Nelson, TN; © 2000-2007.

Hayes, Jimmy L.; Lectures: Election vs Free Will; Can Salvation Be Lost; Andersonville Theological Seminary, GA; © 2006

Hartill, J. Edwin; Principles of Biblical Hermeneutics; Zondervan, MI; © 1947.

Hill, Jonathan; History of Christianity; Zondervan, MI; © 2006.

Kennedy, D. James; Evangelism Explosion; Tyndale, IL; © 1996.

Larkin, Clarence; Dispensational Truth, Larkin, PA © 1918.

Lutzer, Erwin; The Doctrines That Divide; Kregel, MI; © 1998.

Melton, J. Gordon, editor; Nelson's Guide to Denominations; Nelson, TN; © 2007.

Mullins, E.Y; Baptists Beliefs; Judson Press, PA; © 1991.

Nettles, Tom J., editor; Why I am a Baptist; B&H, TN; © 2001.

Olsen, Roger, E.; Arminian Theology: Myths and Realities; InterVarsity, IL; © 2006.

Rhodes, Ron; Christianity According to the Bible; Harvest House, OR; © 2006.

Turner, J. Clyde; These Things We Believe; Convention Press, TN; © 1956.

Various, Biblesoft's, PC Study Bible 4, © 1994, 2003 Biblesoft, Inc. and International Bible Translators, Inc.

MAP and Lyrics

www.freebiblemaps.org

McGuire, Rambo, "I'm Adopted", © 1978 Designer Music/SESAC, Songs Of Rambo McGuire/SESAC

About the Author

Melonie Mayes-Tyler (Doctorate of Theology, and Master's Biblical Studies New Testament from Andersonville Theological Seminary (Camilla, GA); MBA from Oklahoma City University (Oklahoma City, OK); B.S. Management from Jackson State University (Jackson, MS)), is a student and lover of God's WORD and believes in the inerrant WORD of God. Dr. Tyler also understands the importance of knowing, understanding, and applying sound doctrine! Mayes-Tyler has been serving the LORD in a teaching capacity for more than 30 years and has enjoyed writing various curricula for Biblical instruction.

She has been a member of Paradise Baptist Church since she was 7 years old. Mayes-Tyler served as the Youth Director for 15 years, where she taught Bible Study, Sunday school, praise dancing, and theater. She also prepared the youth for Bible Bowl competitions.

Consider securing the <u>Study Journal for Salvation Security, Election, and Free Will</u> which is the companion piece to the book. It is a great item to enjoy while answering questions from each chapter; reflecting on the Scriptures presented in the book; capturing your prayer diary while going through the study; and journaling how this study has enriched your life.

NATIVE BONE
Publishing